LEVI BENKERT

and CANDY CHAND

no greater
LOVE

Tyndale House Publishers, Inc.
Carol Stream, Illinois

Visit Tyndale online at www.tyndale.com.

Visit the Benkerts' website at www.bringlove.in.

TYNDALE and Tyndale's quill logo are registered trademarks of Tyndale House Publishers, Inc.

No Greater Love

Designed by Stephen Vosloo

Edited by Susan Taylor

Library of Congress Cataloging-in-Publication Data

Benkert, Levi.
   No greater love / Levi Benkert and Candy Chand.
      p. cm.
   ISBN 978-1-4143-6308-0 (sc)
1. Church work with children—Ethiopia. 2. Orphanages—Ethiopia.
3. Missions—Ethiopia. 4. Benkert, Levi. I. Chand, Candy. II. Title.
   BV2616.B46 2012
   266.0092—dc23
   [B]   2012000818

Printed in the United States of America

18	17	16	15	14	13	12
7	6	5	4	3	2	1

For Jessie,

my best friend

SOME OF THE NAMES and identifying characteristics of individuals have been changed. Specifics of events, conversations, times, and dates are offered from the author's best recollection. In reality, people do not walk through life with a tape recorder just in case they someday write a book. Memories are not perfect and always include unique perceptions made by the observer.

Contents

Acknowledgments

JESSIE, FOR YOUR UNWAVERING LOVE, your fierce loyalty, and your adventurous spirit. I don't deserve you; I never have, and now that fact is written in a book so you can't tell me I'm wrong anymore.

Nickoli, Luella, Ruth, and Everly (Edalawit), for being the coolest bunch of kids any man could call his own. I can't wait to see what we accomplish together.

Candy Chand, for the thousands of hours you poured into this book. Without you, none of this would have come together. You truly are a great writer. You inspire me.

Our families, who, despite thinking we were crazy, supported us.

Carol Traver, for allowing me the privilege of sharing my story and for the editorial talent you brought to the project.

Yabi, a true superhero. You worked countless hours behind the scenes from start to finish. You are an inspiration and trusted friend. We will forever be grateful for you.

Lale and Gido, for following your passion and helping your people. God has amazing things planned for you.

Rich and Melissa, Micah and Emily, and Joel and

Adrienne, for everything you did along the way. You each gave until it hurt and then gave some more. This entire book could have been just about the selfless things you did for the tribes in Ethiopia. You are wonderful.

All the amazing people around the world who donated to the orphanage and helped rescue the kids who stole our hearts. Because of you, thirty-three wonderful children are alive and well—you gave them a future. Know that your gifts were not in vain.

The Morrell family, for your unending commitment to orphans. Many times I was sure my e-mail updates would scare you away, but you have proven to be faithful. Thank you!

Steve and Stephanie Gregor, for the countless nights you stayed up late to hear us cry over a scratchy Skype connection. You are selfless givers and inspirations. Steve, without your pushing me out the door in the first place, I never would have gone to Ethiopia.

Chinua and Rachel Ford, you guys were the forerunners, the ones who showed us it was possible and stirred our hearts for more. Four kids? No problem! Bring on the airplanes!

Andy Stroud, for your generous assistance. We greatly appreciate your guidance.

Preston Naramore and Eric Dwyer, for pulling us through in a crisis. You are awesome.

The photographers at Pick a Pocket, for the early rescues. We will always remember your compassion.

The Rock of Roseville, for sticking with us and working

through an accounting nightmare and never breaking a sweat. Kenny, you are the best!

Family Mission Center and all the wonderful people who opened their hearts and accepted us into the family.

I feel small compared to all of you—each one who made this book and journey a reality.

—Levi Benkert

†

To Carol Traver, our awesome editor at Tyndale, for quickly catching the vision of this project and for your wise guidance every step of the way; to Susan Taylor, for your gentle editing and your patience, even when I made frantic calls to discuss the word *that*; to Maria Ericksen, for your marketing expertise and enthusiasm; to Christine Showalter, for processing publishing contracts with a speed I've never before encountered; to Andy Stroud, for your generous advice; to Janis Eckard and Heidy Kellison, for your insightful chapter-by-chapter feedback; to the Wahlbergs, for offering me a peek into Bale's joyous, new life; to the Benkert family—Levi, Jessie, Nickoli, Luella, Ruth and Edalawit (Everly)—for your sacrificial spirit serving orphans across the globe; to the One who persistently whispered, "Abyssinian"; and, of course, to Levi, for giving me the opportunity of a lifetime to share such an amazing story. To each of you, I offer thanks.

—Candy Chand

Introduction

THIS BOOK DOES NOT END WELL—or rather, it ends just the way it should but not the way I planned. When I started writing, things were different, and then things changed. What I thought was going to be a book about past struggles and more-recent victories turned into a book about painful transitions and learning to understand the deep redeeming love of God, no matter what we face.

I am told by my editors that this is just the sort of story people love to read, yet good to read and fun to live are very different indeed. I doubt I'll ever stand around a fire pit with friends recounting many of these stories and saying, "Good times." Instead, I am more likely to end up in a heap of tears while my marshmallow is eaten by the flames.

When I think back to this time in our family's life—the drastic transitions, the mistakes, the frustrating unknowns—I see only one constant: God. He was always there—covering mistakes, holding our hands, forgiving blunders, reaching deep into our hearts and healing. And for that, I am thankful.

This is not a book about someone who has it all

together, or even someone who learned every lesson life had to teach him in a short time span and has now grown up and moved on. This is a book about a man who is a work in progress—a work that will never be complete this side of heaven.

I hesitated many times while writing this memoir. I struggled with the fear that my book might not be well received but also that those who dared pick it up and leaf through its pages would view me as a failure, the man they have nightmares about their kids growing up to resemble.

The process of writing each chapter served to uncover more of my missteps, revealing in the perfect clarity of hindsight that I truly had done a heck of a job screwing things up. In the end, or at least for today, I rest in the conclusion that I would rather be known as the fool who told his own story, mistakes and all, in the hope that others might be encouraged when they hold me up as an example and say,

"At least I'm not as messed up as that guy!"

Tomorrow, however, is certain to bring a tsunami of regret over having opened up so deeply in a book for all to read.

Such is life.

Yet the truth remains: God needs no heroes to work for Him. He chooses the broken, the weary, the torn apart, the weak. If our family accomplished good, it wasn't because of us—it was because of Him.

—Levi Benkert

1

THE EARLY MORNING FOG hovered over the grass huts scattered along the Omo River.

In the distance a few women ventured out, gathering sticks to build a fire. Soon the scorching sun would burn across the sky, baking everyone and everything in its path. For the most part the little village was peaceful, except for one small hut where a young woman was giving birth.

But this was not a joyous occasion.

Inside the hut, the distraught woman struggled through labor, knowing that when the baby was born, there would be no celebration. She understood that the events following this birth—like others before—would haunt her forever.

†

"It's a girl." The young woman's husband spoke, if only in a whisper, as he held his tiny infant for the first time. While he used a sharp rock to cut the umbilical cord, his wife's tears flowed freely, running down her cheeks to the dirt floor.

"Take her away," she pleaded, refusing to look into the eyes of her newborn child. "I don't want to see her!" she cried, gesturing frantically toward the low opening in the hut.

Placing a small cloth over the infant's face, the baby's father made his way outside. Crouching in the fierce heat of the morning sun, the man scratched his fingers into the dirt, spit into his hand, and rolled together a small handful of claylike substance.

Brushing the cloth from his daughter's face, he looked into her eyes—for just a moment. The muscles inside him tightened. Shutting off all natural instincts, he methodically followed his well-thought-out plan. Tilting the infant's head back, he opened her mouth and fed her a handful of dirt.

Then, laying her in the dust, he rose to his feet and reentered the hut, leaving his daughter to die alone.

He didn't look back, determined not to watch the helpless babe struggle for breath while the life drained from her tiny body. He knew from experience that within a few moments, it would all be over.

But this time was different.

Unlike thousands of children before her, on this day, for this child, death was not to be.

†

SACRAMENTO, CALIFORNIA: FEBRUARY, 2009

I promise, I never saw it coming. I was in Northern California unwinding the final shreds of my failing real estate development company.

"Don't go too far without me," I called to my children, who were making their way down the sidewalk leading to the park. We'd moved into the downtown neighborhood—a project I had developed—only three months earlier, and we were just settling in.

"Hurry up!" eight-year-old Nickoli called out, as he danced from foot to foot on the newly laid sidewalk.

"I'm coming! I'm coming!" I snapped, a bit harsher than I would have liked. I had always prided myself on being a good dad. I'd even been interviewed in the newspaper as a young entrepreneur who successfully balanced work and family. But lately, I found it difficult to be mentally present.

I knew the distance that was growing between my family and me was wrong. It killed me every time I thought about it, but the truth was, no matter how badly I wanted to be with my kids, I was preoccupied with my deteriorating business. Everything was falling apart, and the fact that

I was failing as a father seemed to pale in comparison with the threat of bankruptcy and the need to lay off employees who'd given everything they had to make the company viable. The dreams I once had for an environmentally friendly urban village, blossoming from blight, were turning into a nightmare of epic proportions.

Over the past four years, I'd seen my development business go from one secretary, who worked out of my garage, to a successful company with fourteen full-time staff and more than a hundred consultants and contract employees. I was heralded as one of the youngest and most successful businessmen in the city, often asked to speak at conferences and events about my thoughts on the market and how I'd become so successful by the age of twenty-six.

Then, with the collapse of the real estate market, I watched the entire business crumble and evaporate to nearly nothing.

The crash had done more than wipe me out financially. It had wiped me out emotionally. I was tired. Tired of putting everything I had into something that was not working. I was tired of stealing time from my three kids, of asking my wife, Jessie, to endure another late night alone while I stood in front of another planning commission pleading for project approval, all the while sensing that no banker in his right mind would fund construction in a time newspapers were calling a "once-in-a-century recession."

That, of course, was on the inside.

Outwardly I put up a positive front, trying to encourage those around me that there was hope the business would survive. But in my heart, I knew it was over. I'd finally come to the realization that I couldn't pay my employees. I also knew there was absolutely no money left to refund to my investors. The truth was, I couldn't pay anyone a dime.

And the guilt was killing me.

I worried about the unknown. I worried about lawsuits and dragging my family through it all. I wondered what things would look like when it was over. And more than once, I realized my life insurance policy made me worth more dead than alive.

Despite all the unknowns, there were a few things I knew for certain: people were going to blame me. They'd say I should have seen this coming. And they'd want answers. The problem was, I *hadn't* seen it coming. And I had no answers. All I knew was that the market had crashed and the equity we once had was gone. To make matters worse, experts were saying, the pain was not over, and the downturn was about to create a wave of home foreclosures across the country, hitting places such as California the hardest. There was no doubt: my Midas touch was gone.

†

"Hello," I said, dropping five-year-old Luella's hand to pull the phone from my pocket and shift my weight to support two-year-old Ruth, who was still in my arms. The kids were silent. They knew better than to be loud when I was on my cell. Especially these days.

I rattled off some budget details to the banker on the phone. He clearly knew the deals were in trouble and was doing everything he could to get as far away as possible before everything collapsed.

"You have to list the property to see what we can get for it," he explained, as he delivered more bad news. The bank had given us a construction loan to build the homes when values were more than triple what they were now, but the loan documents clearly spelled out what we were to do in a situation like this: come up with cash to construct the houses ourselves or sell off the deal for pennies on the dollar and give the bank any leftover money.

We finally made it to the park. I let Ruth out of my arms, and she ran to the rope swing, which Nickoli had already commandeered. It wasn't ten seconds before she got in the path of Nickoli's swinging and was hit in the face with a shoe.

"I'm going to have to call you back," I said, sliding the phone into my pocket and picking her up, leaves and dirt covering her curly brown hair and tears streaming from her eyes.

"What on earth—" I said, flashing Nickoli an angry look.

"I didn't see her," he said, appearing more shaken by the incident than his sister. It took Ruth only a moment to recover as she climbed down from my arms and headed back toward the swing.

My cell rang again.

"Hello," I answered, with the most patient voice I could muster.

"Oh, hi, Steve," I said, surprised to hear from anyone who didn't want money. Steve was an old family friend who had mentored me during my formative teen years. He was now a pastor at a local church, The Rock of Roseville, and was one of the most generous, compassionate people I'd ever met.

"How are you?" I asked, relieved to be talking to someone about anything other than the declining real estate market.

"I just found out a few guys I know are heading to Ethiopia to help with an orphanage project and was wondering if you'd want to join them."

"Sounds like fun," I said, trying to humor him.

"No, really." He almost pleaded. "You've got to hear this. There's a rural tribe there that are killing their children because of some superstition. A group of German photography students traveling in Ethiopia heard about what was going on and, in order to save the kids, worked to build relationships with the elders of one of the villages.

"Levi, they were given a little girl named Bale who was only hours away from being drowned in the river by her own parents. And there are more children, Levi, just like Bale, who are going to be killed if someone doesn't rescue them. These guys I know are heading to Ethiopia for two weeks to assist with the makeshift orphanage. The Rock will be sending funds to help pay for local staff and the basic needs of the kids. We need a couple of people to make sure things go smoothly. Will you go, Levi? Will you help?" Steve asked.

"What good would I be in Africa?" I asked, intrigued and at the same time absolutely sure there was no way I was going anywhere. My business was a disaster, and I was spending more than ten hours a day trying to climb my way out of the hole. A trip to Africa, for any reason, was out of the question.

"Well, you have experience working with orphans overseas, so I figured you could help," he said, recalling my volunteer work with orphans before Jessie and I were married. "I know it's a lot to be throwing at you, so suddenly and all, but why don't you call me back after you've at least thought about it for a few minutes."

"Okay," I mumbled before hanging up, already knowing what my answer would be. I might be daring and adventurous, but leaving for Ethiopia would be crazy. The timing couldn't have been worse.

Still, there was something about Steve that made me consider the possibilities. I'd lost touch with him for almost ten years, but when my business began to fall apart, I looked him up and we reconnected. Remembering how gracious he'd been to me when I was younger, I knew he would provide a compassionate ear during those struggles.

Knowing he was a minister, I had made it clear up front when we reconnected: Jessie and I were not attending church. Frankly, although we were believers, we were tired of what we often saw: lots of people who didn't do enough to help others and, for the most part, appeared way too self-absorbed. Steve never judged us. He didn't even suggest that Jessie and I return to church. He simply encouraged us to seek God, who, he believed, always had a plan.

I had once shared with Steve that I found life uninspiring. "Even when things were going well and we had lots of money, I had to step back and ask myself, *What's the point?* I know that money, recognition, and success aren't the answers, but I have a hard time finding anything else that matters either," I'd told him one evening in desperation.

During our occasional get-togethers, Steve managed to offer a broader perspective on life. He once asked me about my volunteer work in Mexico, India, and Brazil. "Did you feel a sense of purpose then?" he probed, gently trying to urge me in the right direction. "More importantly, Levi, have you thought about whom you're living for?"

†

I spent the next five minutes pushing the kids on the swing while my mind continued to wander. I knew I should call Steve back to give him an absolute no, but instead, I started thinking about what a break it might be to escape to Africa—if only for a couple of weeks. I slid my phone out of my pocket and hit speed dial for my wife. I tried to casually drop Ethiopia into the conversation and then laugh it off, but Jessie immediately set me straight. "You should do it," she insisted.

"Whatever," I said, still chuckling.

"No, really, Levi. Hang up the phone and call Steve back. Tell him you're coming. You can use our emergency fund to buy your ticket."

"No way!" I protested. "That two thousand dollars was set aside in case the absolute bottom falls out. It's our only safety net. It's there in case our family needs it for survival, for things like groceries."

"We'll be fine, Levi. My intuition tells me this is the right thing to do," she persisted. "You need to take a leap of faith."

I fumbled around for a way to respond, but Jessie was so firm that I was at a loss to challenge her. Besides, there was a side of me that desperately wanted to get away, to be alone and then return with a renewed passion for life—and maybe some ingenious ideas for saving the business. "It was while I was on a trip to Africa," I would say when asked how I'd come up with the idea that saved my investors and beat the market. The fantasy flashed before my eyes as I contemplated the beauty of it all. It could work: I would go to Ethiopia, do good deeds, find myself along the way, and come back to do even more good at home. It was well worth the relatively small price of a plane ticket.

"Just call him!" Jessie insisted, interrupting my thoughts before hanging up the phone.

I stood with the cell to my ear, stunned and confused. Maybe Jessie was right, I thought. Maybe I should just go for it.

I began to toy with the idea of traveling to Africa. There was no doubt that I was at a point where I wanted desperately to find meaning in my life. During the past year I had lost my brother to a drug-related suicide and my best friend and business partner to liver disease. Maybe, I thought, I'd find meaning in Ethiopia. Maybe this is just what I needed. My heart sped up slightly as a glimmer of hope—the first in a very long time—flashed through my thoughts.

While I watched the kids on the swings, I wondered what to do. Should I call Steve? Should I say yes?

As if on cue, a flurry of doubts rushed in: why in the world was I wasting time thinking about Ethiopia? There were meetings I was supposed to be attending, failing budgets to deal with, and an office full of people who looked to me for stability. I knew that even hinting about taking a trip at a time like this would be the end of their loyalty.

Then, suddenly, it hit me.

My presence hadn't done a thing to help our company's bottom line. In fact, it seemed the more I tried, the worse things got. The reality was, the verdict had already been delivered: we were going out of business, and I had no power to stop it from happening. Leaving for two weeks to help people was the right thing to do. Afterward, I figured, I would still have time to wrap up all the financial loose ends, and maybe, just maybe, there'd be a way to save everything after all.

Though I feared with everything in me that it might be the wrong choice, that I might regret going, I found myself punching in Steve's cell number. While I waited for him to answer, I thought, *This is it, Levi. It's finally happened. You are now certifiably insane.*

"I'm in," I blurted out as soon as Steve answered, my voice sounding more confident than I felt.

"Great!" he shouted, before rattling off a number for a man named Rich Lester. "You just need to get ahold of this guy. He will fill you in on the details."

After we hung up, I stood still for a while, trying to wrap my head around what I'd just committed to doing. The whole idea seemed crazy. I didn't even know where Ethiopia was, only that it was somewhere in Africa and there were lots of hungry people living there.

†

Over the next few days I began to develop a strange sensation that the trip to Ethiopia might be God's calling. I didn't know exactly how to pinpoint what I was feeling, but there was a quiet sense growing deep inside me that my decision to go had been divinely orchestrated.

One night, after I tried to express my feelings to Jessie, she told me she'd been praying for a long time for something like this to happen. "I don't know exactly what will come of your trip," she whispered, "but somehow I believe it will be good and that you will be changed forever."

Jessie is an amazing woman with great compassion for others. There was a time when we were a young, adventurous couple, ready to take flight at a moment's notice. We'd both shared a passion to help the world's poor and disadvantaged. Jessie and I had even spent a few months in India working with the poorest of the poor. But things were different now. We were in survival mode, with no money or time to give to anyone. The day we'd dreamed of together, the one where we had made so much money we could help people all over the world, had eluded us.

I stood still for a while, trying to wrap my head around what I'd just committed to doing. The whole idea seemed crazy. I didn't even know where Ethiopia was, only that it was somewhere in Africa and there were lots of hungry people living there.

By the look on Jessie's face, I could tell she understood what the failure of the business was doing to me and was desperate to see something, anything, change. Her encouragement seemed to help when I had to tell investors and employees that I was leaving the country—now, of all times.

But it did not help me sleep at night.

I felt as if I were caught between two worlds: one that I didn't understand but was mesmerized by, and another that had me wrapped so tightly in its dark economic clutches that I could hardly breathe.

†

It was nine at night as I sat in a small café waiting for Rich to arrive. Although we'd spoken briefly on the phone, this was the first time we'd had the chance to actually meet. Rich, who was planning the details of our trip, was a young staff member at The Rock of Roseville, the local church that had raised money to help with the orphans who'd been rescued.

From the moment Rich walked into the café, we hit it off. While we sipped freshly brewed coffee, Rich tried to explain what I'd signed myself up for. However, it wasn't until he pulled up a Google Earth map and showed me exactly where we were headed that it actually hit me. We were going to the middle of nowhere.

Rich and I talked excitedly until the café was ready to close and the tired waitstaff more or less kicked us out. But before heading out the door, we had ample time to bond over shared grief. Rich had recently lost his father, and my brother had died less than a year before. It was clear we had a great deal in common. More important, I sensed in my gut that I could trust him.

†

Within a few days we were packed and ready to go. After I kissed Jessie and the kids good-bye, Rich and I headed for San Francisco International Airport and toward the unknown.

My feelings flitted from excitement, to nervousness, to wondering if I'd lost my mind. When it was finally time to board the plane, Rich and I looked at each other, raised our eyebrows, and shrugged. Everything felt surreal. Only days before, we had no idea any of this would be happening.

Once we had boarded, I did what I hadn't done in years. I shut off my cell phone and put it away. It was exhilarating to be on my own. Although I deeply enjoy being a father, there is something about going on an adventure that makes me feel ready to take on the world.

The flight was long—more than twenty hours—but Rich and I kept busy talking about the enormous possibilities awaiting us in Ethiopia. After going over every single thing we knew about the newly created orphanage and the rescued kids, we finally came to the conclusion that we hardly knew anything at all.

†

ADDIS ABABA, ETHIOPIA

"This is it, Levi. All we can do is move forward and see if God has a role for us to play," Rich said, as we finally made our descent, in the dark of night, to the Addis Ababa airport.

Once we left the plane, we got our first glance at Yabi—a short Ethiopian man in his midtwenties—standing in the waiting area with a small sign bearing our names. Yabi had a calm demeanor and a great smile. He seemed unfazed by the fact that he had to wake up at two in the morning to meet our flight. "No problem," he said in clear English. "I do this all the time." Yabi helped Rich and me grab our small bags and then led us to the airport doors.

Once the squeaky exit door slid open and we were blasted with warm, smoggy air, I got the immediate impression of Ethiopia as a country of great contrasts. Before us stretched the capital city, Addis Ababa, a mix of modern buildings alongside rusty metal shacks. The view was nothing at all like what I'd imagined, which was something more akin to scenes from *The Lion King*.

A newer, raised freeway stood prominently in the distance. The cars in the parking lot were a mix of old and new. Many looked as though they had seen their last stretch of road years ago and had now been abandoned for good. And yet parked near a row of dilapidated vehicles was a shiny new Hummer with polished chrome wheels and bumpers.

Yabi showed us to a red, rusty mideighties Land Cruiser. He ran around to the front, opened the door, and grabbed a screwdriver from under the seat, skillfully using the tool to pry open the back door. Rich smiled, then flashed me a quick we-are-really-in-this-now glance as we loaded our stuff into the vehicle.

Yabi drove us to a hotel just a short way from the airport, where we booked a small room with two beds, both covered with stained, yellowish sheets and surrounded by equally grimy walls. To make matters worse, the bathroom smelled as though it hadn't been cleaned in years. I unrolled my sleeping bag and laid it across the top of my mattress, hoping I wouldn't get the bedbugs I was convinced were invisibly crawling all over the room.

One glance out the window revealed a woman who, by the looks of her clothing, was working the streets as a prostitute. She was leaning against a Land Rover with a large image of a machine gun with a red circle and line through it. I quickly shut the window and made my way to the bed and crawled in. Already we'd ventured far outside my comfort zone—and we hadn't even left the hotel.

When the sun came up, I was amazed to discover that the room looked even worse than it had the night before. But Rich and I were too excited to complain.

†

We left the hotel at five in the morning for the two-day drive to rural Jinka, traveling south along winding roads full of potholes. And the potholes were the good parts. They appeared only on the paved path. The rest of the roads were constructed of rough, difficult-to-navigate-on gravel.

When not distracted by the bumpy ride, we took in the incredible landscape. Because the car had no AC, we kept the windows down, giving us the opportunity to feel the world around us. As we drove, kids ran alongside our vehicle, hopeful for a handout of some kind.

We quickly learned our empty water bottles were a choice gift to the local children. Yabi explained that the kids used them to carry water from the rivers and various wells that had been dug by nongovernmental organizations and other aid groups.

While we traveled from the eighty-four-hundred-foot mountains of Addis Ababa to the below-sea-level valleys of the south, the weather turned from mild and cool to a dry heat—a heat like I'd never felt in my life.

The landscape varied from amazing, lush vegetation to dry, barren desert. I observed twenty-five-foot termite hills that towered above the car. There were incredible African acacia trees, the kind I had seen only in movies, and a multitude of bird species perched in the branches. Rich and I were spellbound. Ethiopia was beautiful— more beautiful than the *Lion King* Africa I'd expected to see.

We spent the long ride in the car talking with Yabi, a man with a genuine heart for kids, and the person who had helped the team of photography students who rescued Bale and eight other children. He was passionate about doing what he could for his people and encouraged us not to be afraid but to help him save lives.

†

JINKA, ETHIOPIA

When we finally arrived at the makeshift orphanage, located in a small rented mud house staffed by Ethiopian locals—a couple of nannies, a guard, and a cook—I was so excited to meet the rescued children. But when I did, I about broke into pieces. We were introduced to nine kids with eyes full of innocence—children who had no idea they had been just days away from being murdered by their own families.

I knew what it felt like to love a child. I had three at home. Two by birth, Nickoli and Luella, and our youngest, Ruth, whom Jessie and I had adopted through the California foster care system. I understood what it meant to love orphans, children who did not have families of their own. But standing in that small compound with a tiny mud house in the middle and looking around at nine rescued little ones with longing in their eyes, I knew it was all over for me.

Although the kids were in a safe place for now, a place where they were loved, I was aware it was only a temporary fix. Many of the children had been rescued only days earlier, but there was no long-term plan for their care. The team of photography students who had discovered Bale and had worked over the past two months to rescue all nine of the kids were getting ready to return to Germany. I feared for the children's future once those students were gone. The Rock of Roseville had provided for their initial emergency needs, but I knew people wouldn't feel comfortable sending additional support if there wasn't an independent party on site to ensure that the donations were actually reaching the kids.

Being a father, I understood the level of commitment it would take to provide for their needs. But as I held the babies and watched them play, I also knew I could never go back to America and pretend I hadn't seen their faces. Something broke inside me. Something changed deep down as I wandered around that tiny, dirty compound in the deep south of Ethiopia, holding those precious children, allowing thoughts of their futures and destinies to take over. Perhaps Jessie was right; maybe she knew all along I would never be the same after seeing the kids. Perhaps there was more to this than Jessie or I could have imagined.

Maybe God was at work.

†

Shortly afterward, Yabi introduced us to Simi, a tribal man who'd been a driving force behind the rescues. Simi was committed to the children, but he had little money and knew there was no way he could take on the care and feeding of nine kids on his own.

"I am going to need help and support," Simi told us as we sat at a local hotel sipping Coke from reused glass bottles and eating *Injera*—a traditional food that tastes like a tangy pancake with an assortment of sauces spread across the top.

From the moment I met Simi, it was clear to me that he was a natural leader. He was well spoken and had a powerful presence about him. Even with his broken English, this man commanded attention.

Simi was born into the Kara tribe and early in life was given the opportunity to attend a boarding school in the north. But even as he learned about the outside world, he remained committed to his people. Over the years, Simi returned to his home many times, and after his education was complete, he came back to live in the small village of Duss, where he was hired as a teacher in a government school.

From an early age, Simi believed he would do great things for his people. And he never doubted that the practice of killing children was wrong. For years he had prayed for a way to rescue the innocents. He told us the young photographers were from a small organization called Pick a Pocket, a group based in Germany who took photos around the world in an effort to raise awareness and work to end extreme poverty. Simi believed our arrival and the Pick a Pocket photographers who helped him establish the orphanage were answers to his prayers.

While we sat in the café on wobbly plastic stools, Simi tried to fill in the missing pieces. "Bale was a one-year-old girl considered *mingi*, which translates in your language as 'unclean,' or 'cursed,' because her top teeth came in before the bottom teeth. It was for this reason she was sentenced to death."

Simi didn't allow the shocked expressions on our faces to slow him down. "A child can be declared mingi for three reasons: if the parents are not married, if the parents do not announce to the elders in an elaborate ceremony that they intend to conceive, or if the child's top teeth come in before the bottom teeth. Once the infants or children are labeled mingi, they are murdered to protect the village from evil spirits. The elders teach that if the killings don't happen, the whole tribe will be harmed. It will not rain. Crops will fail. People will die. Although nobody knows the exact number, some believe as many as one thousand Ethiopian children are killed each year because of the mingi superstition."

"Bale was a one-year-old girl considered mingi, which translates in your language as 'unclean,' or 'cursed,' because her top teeth came in before the bottom teeth. It was for this reason she was sentenced to death."

While Simi explained the practice, I felt horrified that something like this could be happening in the world today. Although I had traveled to developing countries before, the concept of mingi was difficult to grasp.

"Why?" I wondered out loud. "Why would any parent do this?"

"Because they live in fear," Simi explained. "They are

afraid of the spirits, because the spirits might get angry at them and hurt the rest of their family. And they are afraid of what the other tribe members might do to them if they do not kill the mingi child."

As I listened to Simi and my world began to expand, I could feel a deep ache inside. In that little café, this strong Ethiopian leader forced me to confront the furthest reaches my mind could comprehend. I knew there were crazy things going on in the world and that not everyone lived or believed as I do, but this was more than I could fathom.

Rich and I listened intently as Simi continued. "The youngest mingi children are left in the jungle to starve or are suffocated by having their mouths filled with dirt. Older children usually have their hands and feet bound and are thrown into the river. That," he explained, "was to be Bale's fate."

Our eyes pleaded with Simi to stop so we could catch our breath, but he went on.

"Except, in this case," Simi said, smiling, "negotiations took place. The photographers helped me save the children. They promised the elders they'd remove Bale far from the village to 'free their people from the curse.' It was not necessary for her to die, they insisted, only be taken away. Reluctantly the elders agreed, allowing Bale's parents to deliver her to us in a canoe, traveling safely down the river—the same river where she was to be drowned."

With a mixture of amazement and gratitude, Simi

added, "Once Bale was rescued, tribal elders allowed eight more mingi children to be released into our care."

Rich and I were on overload. Gesturing to Simi that we'd heard enough, that we needed time to digest what we'd been told, we asked to go back to the compound.

†

Once we had returned to the orphanage, I felt an overwhelming need to be alone. So I excused myself, went into the yard, and stared at the starlit Ethiopian sky, my mind swirling with conflicting emotions: sorrow and joy. Dread and peace. Confusion, and yet a powerful sense of newfound direction.

Bowing my head, I asked God for help.

There was no doubt about it. Hearing the orphans' stories had transformed my heart. But it took more than stories to revolutionize my life. From the moment I'd met the children face-to-face, from the moment our destinies crossed paths, I knew there'd be no turning back.

So, while the little ones were sleeping, I went back inside and made an overseas call to the one person who had seemed to know all along.

"Jessie," I said, "we need to talk."

2

CLOUDS PARTED as our plane made its final descent into San Francisco International Airport. During the exhausting twenty-hour flight, I tried to stay focused, reminding myself that each minute and every mile brought me closer to Jessie.

The excitement I felt about seeing her and getting to share all I'd experienced overwhelmed me. Our marriage had always been a source of strength, growing with each passing year. Jessie was a rock, an incredible mother and wife. And sometimes, it seemed, she could read my mind.

Besides, I was pretty sure we were thinking the same thing: it was time to start packing and head in a new direction—Ethiopia.

Once Rich and I made it through the long lines at immigration and retrieved our bags from the carousel, I felt my heart begin to pound. Rich and I had experienced a great trip. We'd spent countless hours talking about how we didn't want to leave this world in the same condition it was when we'd entered it. We both believed there was a purpose, a driving force, beneath the monotony of life— a purpose we needed to unearth. We talked about our experiences at the orphanage and how we were reeling from a sense of self-discovery.

Even though Rich and I had met only two weeks before our trip, we believed our bond would last a lifetime. The days we'd spent together, the deep spiritual lessons we'd learned, fused an amazing connection. We were clearly on the same path and were being prepared for a new season in our lives, and this trip was only the beginning. That we knew for sure.

Despite the bond I felt with Rich, I was more than ready to see my wife and discuss the future we were now pondering. With poor telephone connections, the limited conversations Jessie and I had been able to have while I was in Ethiopia proved to be more frustrating than productive. But I was able to understand one thing for certain: we were both considering a move that would be either the worst choice we could make—or the best.

As I walked through large sliding doors that marked the end of the immigration area, I saw Jessie's delicate silhouette. Dropping my bags in a heap, I ran toward her. Jessie lit up as I squeezed her tight, glad to be back in her loving embrace.

"I missed you so much," Jessie said over and over as she kissed my face.

"Me too," I told her, holding tighter still.

I watched down the long hall as Rich and Melissa found each other. Jessie and I made our way toward them, arm in arm.

"What a ride!" Rich shouted as we came closer.

"What a ride!" I repeated, knowing that neither of us would ever be able to describe exactly what we'd seen or felt over the last two weeks.

We promised to meet up soon to discuss what we were going to do next, said our good-byes, and then took off in different directions in search of our cars. I was excited to be alone with Jessie and share everything I'd experienced over the last couple of weeks, but the emotions seemed to cram together in my mind, all wanting to come out at the same time. My brain just couldn't decide where to go first.

"Tell me everything," Jessie said as she clasped my hand tightly.

I struggled for words. "It was different," I finally said, knowing that my response was sorely lacking. "The people are wonderful," I added. "It's not what you'd imagine Africa to be. The land is green and lush. It's more remote than anything I've ever seen. Most of all, there's a huge need. I don't know how to explain what it feels like to see so much need, Jessie. It's just overwhelming. And the kids . . ." I said, almost bursting. "The kids in the orphanage are amazing. Everything we'd heard from the photographers is true. It's all true—how the tribes are killing their children. Someone has to help save them, Jessie. Someone has to step up."

"Is it us?" Jessie asked as she attempted to pry into my mind to see where I was headed.

"I don't know. . . ." I hesitated. "I checked my voice mail when I landed, and there were tons of calls from investors who want me in California, who want me to keep trying to recover the projects. I don't know how we could go—"

"Well," Jessie interrupted, "if you stay, can you fix the business?"

"No way," I answered instantly. I'd spent a great deal of time thinking about the answer to that question, long before she'd asked. And it seemed to me that was what it all came down to: if I stayed in America, would it really make things better for anyone, or had the crash already determined the outcome? And by staying, would I only be giving people false hope—in essence, delaying the inevitable?

To be fair, I'd offered up solutions, attempting to fix the crisis. I'd found buyers for projects that were failing and had attempted to negotiate with banks to reduce money owed. But neither idea was working.

The bottom line was that since the crash there wasn't enough equity left in anything we owned. Not enough for the investors. Not enough for the banks. And not enough to pay employees to continue to run the business.

I knew it, and everyone who owned any part of the company knew it too.

"Okay, then," Jessie went on, mapping out her strategy of logic, "if we go to Ethiopia, will more kids be saved?"

I value my wife's insight. Jessie has a way of cutting to the chase, of seeing things clearly, even when I am torn. "No doubt," I replied. "On my last day in Ethiopia, Simi grabbed my arm and made me promise I would do whatever it took to come back and help. He seemed so desperate, Jessie. I gave him my word."

Jessie reached over and lightly touched my shoulder. I took another breath, and then tried to explain more. "Although The Rock funded the initial orphanage setup, the children still have day-to-day needs. The church can't just keep sending money to this vast unknown, to a brand-new organization on the other side of the planet. Contributors will expect some kind of accountability, someone with boots on the ground who they know and trust. If not us, Jessie, who?"

"Then I think we should do it," she said, looking at me for confirmation.

For the next several miles we drove without speaking—the nighttime freeway almost absent of cars.

The tug-of-war in my head was powerful. Yes, I wanted to move to Ethiopia, but dragging my wife and children halfway across the world was a huge decision. Although we could save lives, I didn't want to sacrifice my own family in the process.

My mind began to wander to a conversation I'd had with my friend Chinua just the year before. We'd been walking down the streets of downtown Sacramento when he told me that he and his pregnant wife, Rachel, planned to take their three children to India to do humanitarian work. I was horrified. And I gave him an earful. I told him in no uncertain terms that he was wrong to take his family, that it wasn't safe for children, and that he'd be making a horrible mistake if he went through with his plan. Sure, I'd been to India to work with orphans, but it was long before I had a wife and kids.

The tug-of-war in my head was power-ful. Yes, I wanted to move to Ethiopia, but dragging my wife and children halfway across the world was a huge decision. Although we could save lives, I didn't want to sacrifice my own family in the process.

While I went on and on trying to talk sense to my friend, he stopped dead in his tracks, looked me in the eye, and said, "Rachel and I are taking our family because we believe we're called to India to help the poor. Something could happen to my family anywhere, Levi— even in California. We're going to follow our calling, and right now, our calling is in India."

Because Chinua was so firm, I dropped the subject, but that didn't stop me from thinking he was out of his mind. Now the irony began to hit me: if anyone had told me that just a year later I'd be considering taking my entire family to Ethiopia, I wouldn't have believed it in a million years.

"Well?" Jessie asked, bringing me back from my thoughts.

"Yeah," I said, feigning confidence. "We should do it."

†

Over the next few days the high from being in Ethiopia began to fade, leaving me filled with doubts. I feared uprooting our family and moving to one of the poorest countries in the world. As a husband and a father, I felt responsible for our safety and well-being.

And from a practical standpoint, I wasn't sure we could even raise the money to fly our family of five halfway across the world. Our finances were a mess, and my business was a failure. Oddly enough, we couldn't afford to go or stay.

But in my deepest soul, I sensed that none of that mattered. On the other side of the world there were nine orphans, young children who'd barely escaped death. And they were waiting.

Jessie and I knew we'd have to break the news to our kids, tell them our lives were going to change in a major way and we were about to step into the unknown. We talked about the emotions they would feel and what this would ultimately mean to their world.

Jessie was already homeschooling our two older children, while the youngest, Ruth, was just two years old. But in all cases, there'd be the end of dance classes, the end of study groups, and the end of friendships. One thing was certain: nothing was going to stay the same.

"Is there a grocery store nearby?" Jessie asked one afternoon, out of the blue.

"Yes," I assured her. "I went to one in Jinka. It was about the size of a 7-Eleven. They had peanut butter and crackers—you know, stuff like that."

On the other side of the world there were nine orphans, young children who'd barely escaped death. And they were waiting.

"Did they have milk?" Jessie asked, clearly trying to get her head around the move.

"No dairy at all," I answered, wondering to myself what we would be eating. "Dairy's only available in Addis Ababa. But there are loads of fresh vegetables and fruits in Jinka," I said, trying to sound positive. As the words tumbled out of my mouth, I wondered who I was kidding. The thought of meals made from peanut butter, lettuce, and bananas wasn't about to tempt anyone.

Jessie looked at me doubtfully. It was clear she was having second thoughts. But although I felt the same way, neither one of us was willing to say it out loud.

†

"We need to talk," I said to our three kids as we sat around the dinner table. "We're going to do something new as a family," I explained, trying to calmly approach the major change coming our way.

"You know how Daddy went to Ethiopia and met those kids we saw in the pictures?" Jessie asked.

"Yeah," they joined in quickly.

"Well, we believe we should move to Ethiopia to help rescue more kids and give them a better life," I said, letting the words float across the room.

While our two youngest continued to eat, Nickoli's brow wrinkled and a tear formed at the edge of his cheek. "For good?" he asked, as his emotions started to rise.

"For at least a year, Nickoli," Jessie said, wrapping her arm around him.

"This is what we feel God is calling our family to do," I added.

"But why?" Nickoli asked.

"Well, you know how we explained that the kids are sometimes killed?" I asked.

"Yeah," he whispered, "but what does that have to do with us?"

"I know we'll be giving up a lot, but if we go, we think we'll be able to help rescue more children," I said, knowing I'd never be able to fully explain the situation to someone so young.

Jessie and I tried to direct the topic to items we'd be able to bring with us. "We'll bring your Legos," Jessie promised, knowing how much they meant to Nickoli.

"It's going to be an adventure," I added, with as much enthusiasm as I could drum up.

After some reassurance that life as we knew it would

not, in fact, end and that we'd still be a family no matter where we called home, Nickoli started to come around. "Will we really be able to help the kids?" he asked, finally shifting his focus more to where we were headed than on what we were leaving behind.

"Yes," Jessie said, nodding her head and patting him on the arm.

"Then I think we should go," he said confidently as he stretched his back tall.

Jessie leaned over and kissed Nickoli on the cheek. Within moments, the mood in the room changed as all three of our kids began dancing around the table chanting, "Ethiopia! Ethiopia!"

3

OVER THE NEXT FEW DAYS, my resolve to move to the other side of the world began to deteriorate, especially after meeting with investors to explain what I was planning. They all knew the end was near. The newspapers and TV stations were devoting extensive coverage to the damage that was unfolding in the failing real estate market, and I'd spent the past several months going over the impacts on the business to anyone willing to listen.

Even so, our leaving for Africa was not an option some people wanted to hear about. "Why do you think it's okay for you to walk away from this mess?" one investor argued, as I tried to share my plans over lunch.

"I understand your frustration. I really do," I explained. "But I'm just so tired of trying. For the past two years, I've put everything I have into this. I've used the last of the money I saved, taken out cash advances on my credit cards to pay my employees and interest on the loans. There's just nothing left." I rambled on, trying my best to clarify the situation. "Besides, I'm going into bankruptcy personally; what more can I do? We're at the end of our money, and no investor in his right mind would put dollars into deals that are upside down. It's all a mess. . . ." I trailed off.

The fact of the matter was, things were a lot worse than I'd fully realized. I'm not sure what it was that kept me from telling everyone just how bad it had become financially. Perhaps it was my pride, or my refusal to admit failure.

Although I was honest with investors, early on I'd found myself trying to assure folks that things would somehow turn around. I hated being the one to deliver bad news. Hated telling anyone it was over. It just went against my nature. I'm the kind of guy who likes to fix things, likes to make people happy. It's not my personality to crush anyone's dreams. But I had to admit, I was doing a pretty good job of crushing them now.

†

As I tossed restlessly in bed, I couldn't stop thinking, *This is it. This is the day I'm going to come to my senses. This is the day I'm going to call the whole crazy plan off.*

And then my phone rang. "It's me," a voice shouted.

"Hello," I said, trying my best to sound awake. It was Vanessa, one of our closest friends, whom Jessie had known since fourth grade. After I returned from Ethiopia, I'd shared my experiences with her, and she offered to make the trip to Jinka to hold down the fort until my family was ready for the move. For now, someone from the States needed to be at the orphanage, and Vanessa was willing to give it her all.

I couldn't stop thinking, This is it. This is the day I'm going to come to my senses. This is the day I'm going to call the whole crazy plan off.

"We have a new baby," Vanessa's voice rose, almost singing with happiness. "She's a girl! And she's beautiful! Simi went down south to the tribes a few days ago and came back with her today. She's only a few hours old, Levi. I'm not even sure what her name is yet. All I know is, I'm in love! I can't believe how beautiful she is!" Vanessa was almost hysterical with excitement.

"That's amazing, Vanessa. What happened? Why was she considered mingi?" I asked.

"I have no idea," Vanessa sheepishly admitted. "I only saw Simi for a minute. I'm sure I'll get the details soon. But she's incredible, Levi. She's absolutely incredible!"

Disrupted by a poor connection, Vanessa and I said our good-byes, promising to talk soon. I put down the phone, ran upstairs to our bedroom, and woke Jessie. "We've got another baby," I said, overjoyed. "Can you believe it?"

Jessie awoke with a huge smile across her face.

"Another one, Levi? Really? We can't wait much longer. We need to get there as soon as possible," she insisted, as only a mother could.

"Yes," I agreed, now more confident than ever. I don't know what it was exactly, but hearing about this little baby hit me like a brick. For some reason, this child spoke to more than my heart. This child broke through to my soul.

†

Time was short, and Ethiopia was calling. I tried my best to explain to everyone why we were moving, but few, it seemed, understood. "You're crazy," they'd tell me. "You're only going to last a month," others would say. But the statement I heard the most was, "You don't even have a real plan."

It was true. I didn't have a solid plan. Everything about going to Ethiopia had been a leap of faith. But the truth was, I was tired of planning down to the last detail, only to have things implode anyway. I had started my business with a three-year plan, a five-year plan, and a ten-year plan, and it had been wildly successful. And then, without warning, it all fell apart. If there was one thing I knew by now, it was that none of us can ever really plan our lives—we can only do our best. But sometimes we have to step out into the unknown, to follow our gut instincts, in order to do the right thing—even if doing so flies in the face of logic.

So, between fielding others' criticisms, we moved forward at an incredibly fast pace, applying for visas and getting a series of travel inoculations. We found a local doctor with experience preparing patients for the Peace Corps. We made appointments and offered ice-cream bribes to appease three children who were bound for sore arms. Unfortunately, even ice cream didn't help the feeling of being sick after the yellow fever shot, which made everyone nauseated for a couple of days. Even so, we managed to get through it by keeping our eyes on the goal of getting to Ethiopia and seeing the children.

If there was one thing I knew by now, it was that none of us can ever really plan our lives— we can only do our best. But sometimes we have to step out into the unknown, to follow our gut instincts, in order to do the right thing—even if doing so flies in the face of logic.

Eventually we struggled through meetings with business investors who felt we were abandoning the company too soon, scheduled a huge garage sale to get rid of our belongings, sold our car, prepared to move in with Jessie's parents, said tearful good-byes to family and friends, and, most of all, prayed things would work out.

†

My alarm buzzed at what felt like an ungodly hour. I stirred in bed, trying my best to get up. We'd stayed up late the night before going through the entire sum of our worldly possessions and sorting them into three piles. The largest consisted of things we were going to get rid of at the garage sale. The midsize pile was made up of items that would fit into a storage area a friend let us use. And the smallest pile contained a few necessities we could actually squeeze into our bags and take with us to Ethiopia.

I rolled my way out of bed and swung my feet onto the floor. The sun still hadn't risen, and I was in no way ready to get up. But the craigslist ad had been posted, and I knew there was no way we were going to get rid of so much stuff if we didn't sell it today.

I made my way downstairs, turned on the coffee-maker, and rubbed my eyes—trying to get them to adjust. *This is it,* I told myself as I looked around the room at the large piles all around me. *This. Is. It.*

As I stood there drinking my coffee and staring at the piles in the living room, I felt a strange emotion: before me lay the total of everything we'd accumulated in our nearly ten years of marriage.

At the end of the day, most of it would be gone: we would be letting go—exchanging one life for another—and this was the last step before our great leap into the unknown. I wished for more time, wished I could freeze the clock and ask myself if this was truly what I wanted. But it was too late. The sun was already peeking through little cracks around the curtains, and I had a lot to do.

I exhaled deeply and started with the first box.

†

By just six thirty, hordes of people had arrived. Little did I know that a craigslist ad explaining that my family was moving to Africa and everything must go would attract so many folks. People arrived by the hundreds and managed to clean out almost everything we owned before noon.

Watching the things we'd spent our married life collecting—bookshelves, blenders, stereos, and flat-screen TVs—sold and packed into other people's cars was liberating in a way that surprised me. Oddly enough, as each item that had once seemed so important was carried away, I found myself feeling lighter, as if someone were emptying a heavy backpack I'd been asked to carry around for years.

I felt free.

†

We'd done it: sold, given away, or simply disposed of nearly everything we owned, scaling down our entire lives to what would fit in ten suitcases. Between the sale of personal items and our car, we'd raised enough to fly our family to Ethiopia and had set aside enough for return flights in case of an emergency. With The Rock vowing monthly support for our family's basic needs in rural Ethiopia, we felt as ready as we'd ever be.

I looked at our tightly packed bags on the driveway

and felt stunned, as if the weight of our leaving had hit me all at once. Although the excitement was electrifying, the reality of what we were about to do gave me deep last-minute pangs of uncertainty. I walked back inside and into the bathroom. The reflection in the mirror appeared distant, as if someone I'd never met was looking back at me. I closed my eyes and splashed water on my face. *Think of the kids in Ethiopia,* I reminded myself over and over.

I walked back outside, buckled our children into their safety seats in the borrowed car, and hugged our loved ones good-bye. Then, with all the confidence I could muster, I pulled the car out of the driveway and headed toward San Francisco International.

†

Just six weeks after I'd returned from my short trip to Ethiopia, my entire family was on a plane, heading to Africa. After a twenty-hour flight we landed in the city of Addis Ababa at two in the morning, tired, hungry, and with three exhausted kids in tow.

As we lifted our bags off the squeaky carousel, I allowed myself to face a few hard truths: a part of me knew that moving to Ethiopia was crazy. I'd heard from nearly everyone I knew that we shouldn't go, but until this moment, I'd successfully managed to ignore their warnings. I looked at my tired family and could almost feel them grasping onto me for stability. To them, everything had suddenly gone from known and comfortable to dirty and unstable.

The kids understood why we were here. Jessie and I had spent countless hours explaining over and over what we were going to do as a family in Africa, but none of it had really sunk in. Until now.

While I stood there looking over our bags, strewn around my feet on a dirty airport floor, I realized that I just might go down as the dumbest husband and father in history.

After we managed to locate three wobbly luggage carts that looked as though they had seen decades of abuse, we headed out of the airport.

"What is that smell?" Nickoli immediately asked, as the sliding doors opened and we were blasted in the face with a distinct mixture of diesel fumes and smoke from cooking fires.

"That's the scent of Africa," I said, trying to maintain the high spirits we'd left home with.

"Well, it's stinky," Nickoli replied, holding his nose.

"You'll get used to it," Jessie encouraged, smiling in my direction.

Thankfully, the message of our arrival had made it to our temporary guesthouse in Addis Ababa, and an old Toyota minibus was waiting outside, ready to take us to the much-needed beds we were craving after such a long flight.

In the dead of night we made our way to the guest

home and put our exhausted children to bed. We'd made arrangements to stay in Addis for less than a week before heading out on the two-day drive to rural Jinka. For now, we'd acclimate to Ethiopia and give our kids the chance to get past the overwhelming exhaustion from jet lag.

After everyone else was asleep, I sprawled out on the mattress, stared at the cracked ceiling, and wondered if I'd made the worst decision of my life. Maybe our well-meaning friends and relatives had been right. Maybe this was a huge mistake.

But right or wrong, the decision had been made. We *were* in Ethiopia. And desperate needs were all around us. Though I feared I might be wrong, I hoped that some-how, someway, we'd be able to find our purpose in this foreign land.

†

After six days in Addis, our children were ready to move on. We woke at five to find our kids bouncing around the room, excited to take on the new adventure they'd heard so much about. I peeked out the windows and saw the backdrop of the early morning sun beaming against a group of Ethiopian runners—who were already out en masse. I'd heard about these runners and how well they do in marathons and races around the world. But it wasn't until I saw them for myself, sprinting barefoot at the break of day, that I truly grasped their splendor.

Once we got the children dressed, it was time to leave the north and the city of Addis Ababa and head out on our journey to the rural town of Jinka.

We found ourselves in an old Land Cruiser with the windows rolled down and the hot desert air blasting our faces. Every passing mile seemed to confirm my fear that I was taking my family into the harshest possible place on earth.

As we drove along, pavement gave way to gravel, which eventually gave way to dirt. The car bounced along at a snail's pace while our driver explained the sights around us. He pointed out birds that seemed half the size of the car, and villages with names we could not pronounce that dotted the landscape.

"What are you going to be doing in Jinka?" he asked, as we made our way down our third mountain pass.

"We're moving there to help with an orphanage," I replied, not really knowing how many details to offer.

"For a month?" he asked, his eyes looking me over for some sign of sanity.

"No, for a long time. We plan to live there," I said, now wishing I hadn't told him anything at all.

"But it is dangerous!" he said emphatically. "There are bad people there, and your family will not be safe. Your kids cannot live in a place like Jinka. No one should live in a place like Jinka. Even the people who live in Jinka do not want to live in Jinka," he continued, his tone conveying disdain for our lifestyle choice.

Jessie didn't miss a thing. She leaned in from the backseat, flashing me a weary look.

"People are hungry there," he went on. "They will steal or do bad things to you. You are foreigners, and all they will see when they look at you is money. You will realize the people in Jinka do not want help. Those people need to be left alone," he said, his voice rising. "And the tribes! I have been to the tribes many times. Some of the tribal people are like animals. They will do anything. Some even kill their own children."

I tried my best to explain that we felt we had a calling and wanted to help. I told him we knew about the tribes and the things they sometimes did to their kids. But when I attempted to explain that this was the very reason we had come, he looked furious and nearly stopped the car to turn around.

"You do not know what you are getting into," he pressed. "This is rough country. There are bandits on the roads. Your family will be easy targets."

I looked back at Jessie and could see the fear in her eyes. She was ready to explode. She did not have to say it. She was frustrated with me for not doing more research before we sold everything and traveled halfway across the world. Jessie had put her faith in my knowledge about the situation. She had no experience telling her what this place was like. During the two weeks I had spent in Ethiopia, only three days were in Jinka, and most of that time was at the orphanage with the kids. The truth was,

I didn't know half as much about this move as I thought I did.

Finally it happened. Jessie—my rock—began to crumble. She was tired from our long travels and certain we were headed for one of those war-torn towns you see in movies.

Seeing Jessie cry in the backseat of that Land Cruiser made me realize that all I had really wanted was to get away, to take my family to a new place and leave the frustration of my failures behind. But in doing so, I'd overlooked hugely important details about the place we were headed. I'd made the move sound so good, so selfless, so perfect and wonderful—a plan where we would swoop in and rescue kids who needed us—but the reality was, I didn't have a clue what I was doing.

I began to fear we were going to learn far more about ourselves and how much we could handle than we'd bargained for. As we drove on, I suppressed the emotions that welled inside me—the beginning of admitting who I really was, what motivated me, and who I had become.

†

When we finally pulled into the town of Jinka, a place that we were determined to call home, night was falling. We drove the mile and a half through town until we found a small, dilapidated hotel. The woman at the counter spoke little English and gestured to a small paper on the desk that listed daily rates. It would cost us around fourteen dollars to get a room with two twin beds. Once I agreed, we unloaded our dusty bags from the luggage rack on top of the car and placed them in the small, dimly lit room.

We thanked our driver before paying him for the trip.

"Are you *sure* you want to stay?" he almost pleaded one last time before leaving.

I paused for a moment. The truth was, part of me wanted to load everybody back in the car and head somewhere else. *Anywhere* else. I considered briefly what that would look like. But we didn't have enough money. Jinka was about to become our home whether we liked it or not.

"Yes," I said, exhaling as the words escaped my mouth. "We're going to stay."

4

EXHAUSTED FROM TOSSING AND TURNING, I tightened my back, pressed my body against Jessie's, and shifted my weight to regain a position on the sliver of stiff foam mattress that was my side of the twin bed. It was useless—I wasn't able to get comfortable and had spent the entire night chasing sleep.

Suddenly I heard a hissing sound coming from the direction of the bathroom. I shot to attention. The small Jinka hotel we had checked into the night before with our family of five had been out of water, but the sound behind me indicated it was back on. I lunged out of bed, hoping to put a bucket under the faucet while it was running, but instead of finding the floor, I fell, my feet tangled in a mess of dusty mosquito netting. The sun hadn't come up yet, and I couldn't see anything. I scrambled to my feet, struggling to break free of the net wrapped around my body.

"What are you doing?" Jessie asked in a low whisper from the tiny bed we had been sharing.

"The water," I said, as I stumbled across luggage and clothing strewn around the room.

"What?" she mumbled, still waking up.

"The water. It's on," I repeated, trying to keep my voice down.

When we'd checked in the night before, the woman at the front desk told us the water had been out for three weeks. I wasn't able to understand her completely—something about the tank and the lack of rain—but it sounded as if she said it would be at least another week before it came back on.

Our family had spent the last couple of days traveling by car in the immense Ethiopian heat, and we were starting to smell pretty bad. All we wanted was to stand under some water. Any water. It did not matter if it was cold or hot or whatever. We just needed showers—and we needed them badly.

I found the light switch on the bathroom wall and pushed it several times. Nothing happened. Apparently the power was out as well. I felt my way along the wall to the sink and turned the knob. The knob squeaked, and the pipe hissed. But even with all that commotion, the water refused to materialize. I turned on both knobs and made my way back to bed. "False alarm," I said, as I began to reposition the mosquito net around us.

"Is it always like this?" Jessie asked.

"Probably not," I said, hoping I was right. I finally got the net back in place and pulled the bottom up—just enough to make a small opening I could crawl through.

"Are we going to be okay?" Jessie asked, now fully awake and ready to talk. Our family was finally adjusting to the eleven-hour time difference. Thankfully the kids were starting to sleep better and were no longer waking up at four in the morning. I knew Jessie's questions were coming from deep inside. I knew that she wanted to be able to trust me, that she needed to be assured I had a plan, and that somehow, in the end, everything was going to work out.

Being here—in this small hotel, with our three kids, no water, no friends, and hardly anyone around with whom we could communicate—was hard.

"We'll start looking for a house right away," I said, as I wrapped my arms around Jessie and kissed her forehead. "We'll only be in this hotel for a few days. Then we'll find a home with beds for everyone, so we can get comfortable."

But before I could say more, Jessie asked another question, "Do you think there's really a reason for us to be here? I mean, we're so out of our element, so unable to understand what's going on—how can we possibly be of any genuine help?"

I thought for a second before answering. I knew Jessie needed reassurance. "I think we'll find our purpose. We can learn more about the culture, and at some point, we'll find a way to make a difference."

"But how do you know?" she asked. The sun was starting to come up, and I was beginning to make out the serious expression on Jessie's face. A tear rolled down her cheek. I pulled her close.

"God has a plan," I said, knowing that anything I could come up with, any plan I tried to pretend I had at that moment, would just sound ridiculous. The real truth was, I had no idea what was going on. I had no idea whether we were really wanted in Ethiopia, and I was just as scared as Jessie. I knew we had given up everything for this cause. We no longer had a home, except a temporary stay in this hotel—a dirty, stinky, dingy hotel in the middle of nowhere—in the far south of Ethiopia.

Jessie returned my embrace and pushed her face against my neck. "I know He has a plan," she said. We spent the next hour in silence—two people, side by side on a tiny bed—staring off into space. This was the deepest, darkest place we'd ever been together and yet, strangely, at the same time it was one of the most beautiful places we'd ever been. We were at that sacred place of human weakness, where we recognized that our abilities were not enough. We had no choice but to trust God.

†

As if on cue, the twin bed three feet to the right of us stirred. "Can we go to the orphanage now?" our kids asked, having waited long enough to meet the children they'd come so far to help.

"Don't you want to eat first?" Jessie asked Nickoli, who was already rummaging through his bag in search of something to wear.

"I really want to see the kids," he said, his words filled with excitement and nearing a scream.

"Okay then," Jessie agreed, as she untangled the mosquito net for the fifteenth time since we'd arrived. We quickly put clothes on the kids and headed toward the hotel exit.

I hoisted Ruth onto my shoulders while we made our way out of the hotel compound and into the dusty streets of Jinka. As we stepped onto the dirt road, a bus buzzed by, blasting a strange horn that sounded like a cross between a fire engine siren and an ice-cream truck.

Within moments, we had amassed an entourage of street children, all of whom wanted to hold our hands and use what little English they knew to communicate.

"Are you fine?" they asked as we walked quickly down the road. "I'm fine," they would reply in response to their own question. It was clear they didn't know what they were saying any more than we grasped their native Amharic.

"Can you hold me?" Luella asked, looking at me with pleading eyes—her voice revealing she was on the verge of tears.

"Why?" I asked, stooping down to her level to see what

was going on. Immediately several kids surrounded me and began to pat my head. I quickly realized they had been touching Luella's long blonde hair as we walked and she felt a bit overwhelmed. Luella squinted, as if she could hold back the tears by squeezing her eyes closed. She pulled her head sharply to the side as another child reached out to touch her golden hair. Jessie took Ruth from my shoulders while I lifted Luella up to a safe place where she could watch this new world from a cautious distance.

†

By the time we reached the rusty corrugated-metal gate that surrounded the small orphanage compound, we looked as if we were leading a parade. We arrived with more than twenty children, many of whom sang and danced as we walked.

Although the kids who accompanied us were excited, we were not the first foreigners they had seen. Jinka was becoming a hub for tourists who came to see the many tribes that lived in the mountains and valleys. The tourists would often give candy or money to the children, and they had learned quickly that taking a walk with a foreigner could be profitable.

I knocked at the metal gate, waiting with anticipation for someone to answer. Within seconds, Gude, a tall Kara man with a sweet smile, arrived. Gude was the groundskeeper/guard for the orphanage. He and his wife,

Hiwot, who was the house cook, lived on the compound. Besides Gude and Hiwot, the orphanage was staffed by two local nannies. I'd met the Ethiopian workers on my recent trip with Rich and was impressed with their kindness toward the children.

"Hello, Levi," Gude said, as he swung the gate open and embraced me with the typical Ethiopian greeting—a handshake and shoulder bump. It's sort of like a hug, but both of your right shoulders bump together. The more times the shoulders bump, the more you express your affection and happiness at seeing the other person.

"Hello, Gude," I said, doing my best to return the complicated greeting. We tried to have a brief conversation, but within a few moments, he had reached the end of his English vocabulary. So we moved on to the rest of the local staff, who were now assembled excitedly just inside the gate.

After spending a few moments introducing ourselves, we were invited into the house to meet the nine rescued children and one tribal mother, Chowki, who'd come to the orphanage to temporarily live with her mingi son, Abreham.

In an instant Jessie stooped down to pick up Kulo, an outgoing three-year-old boy. She flashed me a quick smile. Without a doubt this was her element. Jessie was born with a heart for kids and had a way with them like no one else I've ever known. Even the most hostile child melts in Jessie's arms.

†

I sat on the ground and allowed the kids to climb all over me as our youngest daughter, Ruth, clung to my side. The ruckus seemed to be more than she could handle.

One of the nannies, Zeritu, was sitting in the corner, near what I thought was a pile of blankets. She smiled, then gestured—encouraging me to come closer for a look. When I approached, I realized that this was not a pile of blankets at all but, rather, a baby girl.

This tiny infant had the most beautiful face. She was the darkest of the children in the orphanage, with lips that were almost purple. Zeritu motioned for me to pick her up. I stooped down, lifted the little baby close, and fell instantly in love. She could not have been more than five or six pounds, her tiny frame almost lost in my arms. She looked up at me for a brief second, and then closed her eyes. She did not squirm, did not try to get away, but rather burrowed securely into my chest.

Jessie walked over and looked at the small package I was holding.

"She's perfect," I said.

"Wonderful," Jessie agreed, bending down to kiss her on her small, round cheek. There was something about holding a child this little, this new—something about knowing she had so recently been doomed to death only to be rescued at the last second—that overwhelmed me.

Handing her gently to the nanny, I walked over to

a small bench in the corner of the orphanage and sat down. I smiled as I watched the animation of my kids, who were running around the center of the room trying to teach their new friends to play a rousing game of Duck, Duck, Goose.

†

While the kids ran around, the staff gave Jessie and me a tour.

The condition of the orphanage was beyond substandard. The walls were filthy.

Just off the courtyard was the bathroom, a small room with a twenty-foot-deep hole in the floor. It smelled horrible. There was no running water. The door was broken on the toilet stall, so it was necessary to squat while staring at people who were just a few feet away. Flies buzzed everywhere.

A few paces away from the toilet was another hole in the ground—this one a well. Jessie and I looked at each other, both clearly wondering the same thing: was this the same water coming out of the ground that had just been deposited in the toilet?

In the corner we saw another hole, this one used for burning trash. It was located right next to the play area.

Jessie and I began to clean. We scrubbed everywhere until we were exhausted. Then we began basic repairs. Once we'd done all we could, we noticed Abreham had a horrible rash.

I took him to one of the nearby town clinics and was told he had a bad case of scabies. They gave me a medicated cream, and after returning to the orphanage, I took him aside and, following the clinic's instructions, scrubbed Abreham's skin. As Abreham cried and the nannies watched nervously from a distance, I did my best to reassure this sweet little boy, in a language he did not understand, that I was only trying to help.

Once Abreham's treatment was complete and I'd dressed him in clean clothes, I looked for a stuffed animal to return a smile to his face. It was then Jessie and I noticed that many of the toys we'd sent to the orphanage were sitting high on a shelf where the kids could not reach them.

We began to rearrange the rooms to clear a space for a playroom, bringing the toys down to the level of a child's reach. After cleaning up and moving things around to make it work, we tried our best to explain to the nannies that this was a place for the kids to play. But immediately they took out a key and locked the door to the room we'd just set up, not allowing the kids to go in at all.

It was clear to Jessie and me that the nannies loved the children, but they had a sense that nice, new things—the kinds of things they'd never seen before—were to be preserved rather than used and enjoyed.

Although the orphanage was a safe place for the rescued mingi children, at this point it was far from being the home we knew they deserved.

†

After spending hours caring for Abreham; holding and playing with the other kids; changing diapers; and cleaning, repairing, and reorganizing the orphanage, and still not scratching the surface, we said our good-byes for the day, swung Ruth and Luella onto our shoulders, and started back toward the hotel—joined once again by a parade of dancing children.

"Why do the parents want to kill their kids?" Nickoli asked as we walked along the road. Before we left the United States, Jessie and I had tried to explain, in the simplest terms, the mingi practice. However, seeing the children for real, up close and personal, magnified our kids' perceptions.

"They don't want to kill their children," Jessie said. "They love their kids, just like we love you guys, but they live in a place where the fear of evil spirits is very real. They kill their children because they're worried about what might happen if they don't. They are worried that all their kids will die if they don't kill the child they believe is cursed."

"Do they really kill them?" Luella jumped in, still amazed that the nine children she'd just met had actually been sentenced to death.

"Yes," I said, pausing to try to figure out some way to make this intense reality less grown up and more on her level. "But they're safe now," I reassured her. "Safe and sound. And we are here to do everything we can to love these kids and make sure they stay safe forever."

Once we got back to the hotel, we dined on roasted chicken—a meal that was so fully cooked, it nearly took pliers to pull it apart—then settled our children into bed. Weariness hung heavily over our family, and the emotions of meeting the kids in the orphanage and seeing the tiny town we intended to call home were difficult to absorb.

And there were more concerns. We'd been informed that an Ethiopian law—something akin to affirmative action in America—requires any organization working with tribes to be headed by someone from the tribe. Although on the American side a nonprofit could raise funds for the children, ultimately the Western board could never fully control the organization. If there was a difference of opinion, all final decisions would need to be made by the Ethiopian director. This put us at great risk. Although Jessie and I had given up everything to come to Ethiopia, we now realized that at any moment the children in the orphanage could be removed from our care.

Jessie and I closed the door to the hotel room and sat on the concrete floor with our backs against the wall. Too stunned to talk, my wife placed her hand on top of mine. We were each processing more emotions than we were able to express. Indeed, there was a need for us to be here; the lists we'd created in our heads to help the kids and make the orphanage a better place were a mile long. The real question was whether we could handle living in a place like Jinka.

†

After fourteen days in the hotel with no water and with power that seemed to be off more than it was on, we finally moved into a small house near the orphanage. It was a bright red mud house with a tin roof, cement floors, and a pleasant yard full of tall eucalyptus trees that swayed in the wind.

Surrounding the yard was a wall made of bushes and trees. The owners had run barbed wire through the shrubs to create a barrier to the outside world. It didn't work. The holes served as windows for the countless neighborhood children who spent their afternoons staring at our kids while they played outside and watching our every move as though we'd just landed from another planet. We had moved to our small abode with no furniture except for a few tents that we used to keep the malaria-carrying mosquitoes away at night, when they come out in full force.

Within a few days we had settled in and hung a hammock between two trees so we could swing gently back and forth, allowing our minds and bodies to adjust to the slower pace of Africa.

†

"I can't eat another bite!" Nickoli cried out as he slammed his flimsy plastic camping spoon onto the floor. "We've had cabbage and carrots every night for the past week," he went on, tears flowing from his eyes.

I glanced at Jessie to see her reaction. She looked as if she might start crying too. "I know," she answered, placing her arm on his shoulder. Always more patient than me, always able to see the heart, to feel the pain, Jessie tried to comfort Nickoli. "We're doing our best to give you guys good food, but it's not easy to find what you like here."

We sat in silence for the rest of the meal, while we each tried to stuff one more bite of the bland morsels into our mouths, just enough to fill our stomachs and get us through another day without triggering hunger-induced headaches.

After dinner I closed my eyes and began to wonder, *What am I doing to my family? How can I possibly watch my own kids struggle to eat just enough food to keep healthy?* Things were so bad that my children had even started to lose weight.

I knew our struggle paled in comparison to the starving families we saw all around us. Yet this didn't have to be our reality. This didn't have to be our battle. We were here to help the suffering. Not to join them.

I thought back to the large solid-wood dining-room table we had sold at the garage sale back in America— the one we used to sit around and recite clichés to our children: "Do you know how many hungry kids there are in Africa? Eat your food!" And now here we were, eating another measly meal of cabbage and carrots on the floor of our African mud house. The irony hit me: *My own children had become hungry kids in Africa!*

In the silence that had filled the room, we all seemed to have come to the same conclusion. I struggled to find words. I wanted to give a rousing speech about why we were here and all the good we were doing with the orphanage and the rescues. Yet the reality was, we had spent the past few weeks just getting our family settled, and hardly anything else had been accomplished. We had no furniture, except for a few mattresses, no way to cook food, except for a small coal burner that took nearly an hour to warm up. Our family was a wreck, culture shock was starting to set in, and we all felt lonely.

I thought back to the large solid-wood dining-room table we had sold at the garage sale back in America— the one we used to sit around and recite clichés to our children: "Do you know how many hungry kids there are in Africa? Eat your food!" And now here we were, eating another measly meal of cabbage and carrots on the floor of our African mud house. The irony hit me: My own children had become hungry kids in Africa!

We had nothing to remind us of home and virtually no communication with the outside world. The few times we were able to get through to anyone back in America, we were able to talk for only five minutes before we lost the connection. We felt as though everyone had deserted us. We had made it to the end of the earth, and no one, it seemed, cared that we were here.

The world back home, the place where I had made

that fateful call, the one where I had made the choice to move here, to blow up our lives, seemed only a fairy tale. I knew the choice had been mine, knew I had wanted this and had done everything in my power to make the move happen. But now that I grasped the rest of the story, understood the pain it was causing my family, the struggle for survival we had to endure, I knew better.

A gnawing fear grew inside me. They had been right—the people, the friends and family who tried to warn us not to come to Ethiopia. They had been right—every single one of them.

†

At four in the morning the phone rang. Startled, I got up, staggered forward, and rubbed my eyes, trying to focus on the flashing number. I did not recognize it, so I hit the silence button and made my way back to bed. A few moments later, the phone rang again. This time I looked closer and saw it was an American number. I picked up the receiver and walked outside, where I could create some distance from the rest of my sleeping family.

"Hello?" I said, trying to sound awake.

"It's Manny," a stern voice replied on the other end of the phone. My heart sank. Manny was an investor in one of my real estate development projects before the downturn brought economic devastation. Huge potential profits had quickly turned to losses. Big losses. And we both knew the property was likely to sit for years—even decades—until the money he'd invested would come back to him.

Before we left for Ethiopia, I'd given up my ownership. I would rather have the investors benefit when the market finally came around than try to hang on myself. Besides, I knew I wouldn't be able to put up my share of the property taxes anyway. There was no use pretending I could bring any value to the deal any longer.

"I'm very angry at you for leaving me like this," he started in, his voice conveying the depth of his frustration. "Are you stealing money or something?"

The phone shook in my hand as I repeated the word in a haze of disbelief: "Stealing?"

"Listen up—I've been looking over the paperwork, and I don't like this project. I don't like that you're not here, and I especially don't like that you left and ran off to Africa. What is this?" He swore, and his voice rose to a near yell.

"I don't understand," I said, struggling to find the meaning behind his phone call. I thought we had wrapped things up; he knew what I was doing, knew what had happened with the market. No one could have missed it. It was everywhere you looked: the papers, TV. The real estate market in California had dropped by more than 40 percent. This was no smoke-and-mirrors illusion. Everything we had was wiped out. Everything.

"You listen up," he insisted. "I'm going to look into

things, look at all the accounts, and I'm going to find out what you did. I'm going to see just why you felt the need to fly halfway across the world to get away from this mess you made. And if I find anything you did wrong, I'm going to come after you with everything I have. I'm going to make sure you are done. Do you hear me?" he yelled.

The phone went dead. I lowered it far enough to see the word *disconnected* flashing in block letters. I slid my back down the base of a tree, until my body rested in the dirt. My stomach ached, and my muscles began contracting and heaving.

"You listen up," the caller insisted. "I'm going to look into things, look at all the accounts, and I'm going to find out what you did. I'm going to see just why you felt the need to fly halfway across the world to get away from this mess you made. And if I find anything you did wrong, I'm going to come after you with everything I have. I'm going to make sure you are done. Do you hear me?"

He is wrong, I told myself, knowing there was no truth to what he was saying, no validity to his statements. Yet the accusation, the thought of someone trying to find something I had intentionally done wrong, some theft or misconduct, drained the last bit of energy I had left in my body.

This was supposed to be the turning point, the end of the struggle that had been my life for the past few years; instead, things just kept getting worse. Not only was my family in a foreign land, experiencing the culture shock that comes with such adjustments, but back home my reputation had gone from failure to suspect.

"Fraud? Criminal?" I tried out the words for the first time. Tears stained the red dirt beneath me. Deep, painful tears.

5

SCRATCHING THE TEAR-STAINED DIRT, the red clay gathering beneath my fingernails, I sensed the truth of my failures penetrating the layers of my soul. There was no denying it anymore. I came to a sickening realization: I hadn't moved to Ethiopia just to help the orphans of Africa, to make the world a better place, and to obey God's call on my life. The truth was, I'd also moved to Ethiopia to run away.

And in doing so, I'd put my family at risk.

How could I justify my choices? I wondered. How could I think of myself as a man of integrity when I was really just a selfish jerk, parading my family around like a flawless picture of humanitarianism.

My tears mingled with a mist of Jinka rain. I leaned forward and put my hands on my knees, trying to silence the sobs. I didn't want to admit who I'd become. Until now, I'd convinced myself that God was directing my path, showing me the way. But now I was beginning to face the truth about my inner turmoil.

The investor's call had brought me to the bottom, ripping away my shield and exposing the deep pain in my heart. Manny was wrong about the business; I hadn't stolen anything. But he was right about one thing: I was running. I hadn't come to Ethiopia because I was this wonderful man who wanted to help people in need. I came to Ethiopia because *I* was a person in need.

A flash of lightning illuminated the yard, followed by a tremendous clap of thunder. "I'm sorry!" I shouted to the darkness. "I'm sorry! I want to be a better man. I want to do good with my life—really do good with my life!"

As I squatted in the dirt, I felt crushed by the weight of my failures, as if the wallpaper had been torn off and my true self were finally exposed, ugly and unworthy.

Then quietly, gently, I began to sense the compassion of God reach deep into my soul. To my amazement, He didn't cast me away. Instead, I experienced the warmth of forgiveness and a distinct certainty that there was a genuine purpose for my life. In that place, that bottom-of-the-ocean place, God met me. I was surprised to discover that I hadn't found Him on the mountaintops of my successes or in the height of my abilities, but in the depth of my despair and failure.

I stood up from the wet earth beneath me. I had no idea what would come next, no idea where to go or what to do when the sun came up. But in that moment I knew one thing for sure: everything was about to change.

†

The little pot rumbled as the water began to boil—minuscule bubbles, slowly rising to the surface, the heat of the coals on the small burner not enough to induce much more than a simmer. I wrapped my hand in an old T-shirt, grabbed the vessel, and poured the water into three small bowls of oatmeal from the local market. The green tin that once held the white oats sat empty in a pile of garbage: Snickers wrappers, a mango skin, the leftovers from last night's dinner of beans and rice.

I carefully dug a spoon into a nearly empty jar of amber honey, wiping away the remains of a bee. "It's ready," I called out to the yard where the kids had been playing in the dirt with a small pile of bottle caps—wholly contented, fully engrossed in their simple game of pretend.

They came running, bright and cheery. It was only seven thirty in the morning, yet their faces were already smeared with dirt, their clothes caked in dusty red earth.

This is contentment, I thought. Ethiopia was burrowing into all of us, massaging our weary hearts

To my amazement, God didn't cast me away. Instead, I experienced the warmth of forgiveness and a distinct certainty that there was a genuine purpose for my life. In that place, that bottom-of-the-ocean place, God met me. I was surprised to discover that I hadn't found Him on the mountaintops of my successes or in the height of my abilities, but in the depth of my despair and failure.

and teaching us what it meant to slow down and take life in—really take it in. I felt the fog of our previous existence begin to lift, to be replaced with something entirely new, clear, beautiful.

Jinka, the small, dusty town in the deep south of Ethiopia, was beginning to teach us how to live. Maybe, I thought, the life we had back home, the one with all the voices, the phone calls, the interruptions, the racing around just to survive, was not really living at all.

"Thank you," the three dirty ones said in unison. I smiled at my children, noticing the innocence in their eyes, the beauty of their tender love, the wonder of their trust.

In me.

Dirty toes lined up, biggest to smallest along the floor, wiggling in the air, happy to be free, away from the confines of shoes and socks. I breathed deeply.

Jessie's warm arms wrapped around me from behind, and I smiled. Ribbons of yellow danced across the floor, shaking with the shadows of thousands of eucalyptus leaves moving in the breeze. I turned to face my wife, embrace her, let the moment wash over me.

This is freedom, I thought. *This is life.*

†

The creaky, corrugated-metal gate scraped the floor as I pushed it open, stepping onto the dusty street outside our compound. A hunched man shoved his hand toward me.

"Please," he begged.

I'd seen him before. He'd recently discovered our house and had set up camp outside our gate in the hope that we'd take pity on him. I paused, looked in his eyes, and for a moment grasped the pain of his existence. I said a prayer, knowing that without a miracle, there was little hope, little chance he would ever be more than a beggar on the street. I went back into the house, gathered up a few remnants from last night's meal, and spread them out before him.

Interrupted by a ringing phone, I walked back inside, picked up the receiver, and said hello. I recognized the man's voice immediately. It was Manny. I swallowed hard—fearing what was coming next.

His words were flying so quickly, I could hardly keep up. Then, it hit me: Manny wasn't mad at all; he was trying to make amends. He told me he was going through an assortment of financial and personal problems and hadn't meant to take it out on me. He knew the business failed because of the market and that none of it was really my fault.

I was at a loss for words. Stuttering for a moment, I thanked him for his kindness, for his understanding. Then, with a fading phone connection, we wished each other well and said our good-byes—grateful for new beginnings.

†

Flagging down a motorcycle, I negotiated a price with the driver to take me into town. We agreed on three birr, about seventeen cents. I slid my body close behind his sweaty physique, trying to breathe from my mouth. He smelled as if it had been at least a week since he'd bathed in the river.

As we sped toward town, I was grateful for the rush of clean air that blasted my face. A few minutes later I voiced my appreciation, slid off the motorcycle, and handed him a little more than we'd negotiated—five birr.

All around me there were people walking, carrying loads of goods to sell at the Saturday market. I knew they'd come a long way. It was overwhelming to see that many people working so hard for so little.

A small woman glanced at me, offering a smile as she juggled several glass bottles of corn alcohol intended for market. She paused, put the bottles on the ground, and came closer.

"One birr," the woman said, hand outstretched in expectation. It was obvious—I was still viewed as an outsider, a tourist passing through, a foreigner with money.

Declining, I headed over to the small grass hut where I'd already been disappointed three times that week. "No connection," the young dark man had said every time I entered the compound. But this time he smiled, welcoming me into the dim room where a Dell computer sat in the corner on a rickety wooden table. "Morning, connection come," he announced, smiling from ear to ear.

I listened with anticipation as he tried to explain

that to make things work, I needed to pull the monitor forward with one hand while using the other to type. I looked at him, puzzled, until he demonstrated. As soon as he let go, the power cut off, and the screen went black.

"Got it," I said, placing my palm on top of the monitor and pulling downward as the screen flickered to life.

After several unsuccessful attempts with the dial up, I finally saw the word I'd been waiting for: *connected*. I exhaled, unsure if I was really prepared for what I might find. This would be the first time in five weeks that I'd had an opportunity to check my messages.

I struggled to type the web address with my free hand, pausing for a second before hitting Enter, and wondering if I'd be better off remaining lost in a blissful sea of ignorance. Going for broke, I pushed the button and waited. After a few moments, words began to float across the screen. "It appears you are trying to access Gmail from a slower connection. Would you like to turn on simple browsing to view your in-box?"

I clicked OK and held my breath: "INBOX—157 Unread Messages." I waited for the screen to finish loading, then scrolled my way through the e-mails, my stomach twisting with anticipation:

> E-vite to a Guacamole Party—*Skip*.

> Party to Toast the Mayor of Sacramento—*Skip*.

Gradually my eyes fell on a couple of messages from my investors. Clicking on the first e-mail, I squinted, then slowly began to read:

> Hi, Levi,
>
> . . . Was wondering when you are coming back? I saw your blog on the L J Urban page . . . no water for 30 days and no electricity for 22 days? Sounds like heaven. Yikes. But what an uplifting experience to be making a difference in these kids' lives. . . . They are so lucky to have you there. . . .
>
> Send me an e-mail if you get a chance. Am managing to hang in there, but just barely.
>
> James

Smiling, I clicked on another:

> Levi . . . it *was* the market, and loss of value that killed us. I am not sure that anything could have mitigated what happened. Maybe lease-optioning would have worked, but that's hindsight. . . .
>
> It was still the guys on Wall Street with the subprime shenanigans that killed everything. . . .
>
> So, keep up what you are doing; do an exceptional job of it; and return to where you left off when the market changes.
>
> Good luck,
>
> Seth

I read the e-mails several times before I really understood the gift I'd been given. I closed the screen and slid my chair back from the desk, dumbfounded. Without a doubt, the messages were an answer to prayer.

As I made my way back to our house, I fumbled for words to explain to Jessie. I tried to describe what it felt like to receive that kind of encouragement. Over the past few days we'd discussed all sorts of horrible possibilities: lawsuits, traveling back home to dig through files to prove my innocence. None of it was good. None of it made us feel we could really settle into Ethiopia.

And now this!

This was a second chance, a chance to continue on and start fresh. Not only had Manny made a turnaround, but there were additional messages reminding me that the investors understood that the market crash had not been my fault.

I'd felt guilty. For everything. Replaying in my mind different scenarios, other routes we could have taken that might have saved everyone from such financial hardship, I wondered. *If only I had known. If only we'd sold everything the year before the collapse.* But with these simple e-mails and the phone call from Manny, I felt free.

†

The next few weeks, Jessie and I danced in freedom. We spent afternoons playing with the kids at the orphanage, discovering more of their backstories and learning to love each one of them.

We spent evenings walking through town, taking in the sunsets, letting the silence soothe our hearts. I began to breathe deeply for the first time in my life.

Jessie and I built relationships with the local staff at the orphanage, learning their names and visiting some of their homes. We fell in love with these wonderful people who were so willing to help, so eager to be part of the solution for a plague that had haunted their tribes for generations.

There were nearly 130,000 people of the Kara, Hamar, and Bena tribes, and although many had long since given up the practice of mingi, countless others still continued, resulting in more children being killed each year than we could imagine. Jessie and I felt overwhelmed, trying our best to understand how someone could love a child—dearly love a child, just as we did our own—and then decide to kill that child because of fear.

†

Luella finished her breakfast of sweet mango while a wild monkey perched on a kitchen chair, reaching for her bounty. Cautious at first, she placed pieces of succulent fruit on the table, just within its reach, then grabbed her flip-flops and skipped toward the door.

As I washed the morning dishes, Jessie rounded up

Nickoli and Ruth. Then, together, we set out for the orphanage.

The moment we arrived, we were greeted by the usual barrage of children wanting to play and be held. Like any child in the world, these kids crave attention and are eager to spend time with anyone who will show them love.

In the corner an infant slept in a small wooden bed. Jessie walked over and found her resting in a puddle of milk. The nannies had placed a bottle in the babe's mouth, and the contents had spilled. Jessie picked her up, only to discover the little one soaked in urine.

We felt overwhelmed, trying our best to understand how someone could love a child—dearly love a child, just as we did our own—and then decide to kill that child because of fear.

Looking across the room, I saw a tear form in Jessie's eye. She'd always had a soft spot for children and had spent several summers while in high school volunteering at an orphanage in Mexico. But something more was going on. It was obvious that Jessie was drawn to this child. I could see it in her eyes.

"What's her story?" Jessie asked Simi as children stirred around our feet and tried to climb our legs.

"She's from Labuk, a small village just a short way from where I was born," he explained. "She was mingi because her mother and father had not held the proper ceremony before they conceived, a ceremony where they would announce their intent to have another child. She has other siblings, but the others are not mingi."

"Then how did she survive?" Jessie persisted, still struggling to understand the full extent of a practice that would cause parents to kill their child.

"Right after she was born, the father took her outside and stuffed dirt in her mouth," Simi said, almost devoid of emotion. Simi had grown up with these stories; some of his own siblings had been killed because of mingi. He was past the pain. This was a part of his life. Yes, Simi was fighting it. Yes, he wanted to stop the practice. But the fact of the matter was, the superstition of mingi was reality in his culture. Such things happened every day. In order to do his work, he had to stay strong.

Jessie stroked the baby's face, holding her tight. I looked on, perplexed that this child could actually be here, safe in Jessie's arms, and only five weeks earlier have been placed outside her parents' hut with dirt in her mouth, gasping for oxygen.

The older children continued to swirl around our legs in happy, playful movements.

"Dirt?" Jessie asked, her voice cracking.

"Yes, but a villager, Ayike, walked by just in time," Simi continued. "He knew about our orphanage. Ayike does not believe in mingi. He took her, cleaned the soil from her mouth, and then ran to another hut and hid."

"That morning, I had a dream," Simi shared. "In that dream, God told me there was a girl in Labuk, a small mingi baby who needed to be rescued. I woke up at four and found a car with a driver to take me there. The driver was not happy, but I pushed very hard, and he finally agreed.

"When I got to Labuk and opened the door to the car, Ayike was standing there. He had the little baby in his arms and gave her to me. As soon as we drove away, I knew what her name should be. I called her Edalawit."

"What does her name mean?" Jessie asked in a hushed voice, keenly aware of the sacred nature of the moment.

"The lucky one." Simi smiled. "Her name means the lucky one."

†

Beads of sweat ran down our foreheads, dripping onto our already soaked clothes. Jessie and I found two empty spots in the tiny living room and sat down. A platter, overflowing with popcorn, was passed our way. A few moments later, another came by—this one filled with sliced passion fruit. We sucked out the juicy insides, savoring the much-needed refreshment.

Jessie and I weren't used to this kind of heat—even in Africa. Simi's house faced the evening Jinka sun, with no trees to serve as a break from the scorching temperature. The mud walls and tin roof did little to protect the home and instead soaked up the sun, creating an ovenlike environment for those who dared go in.

We dared.

Besides, it would have been rude not to go—that much we knew about the culture. If you're ever asked to come inside someone's home and share a meal, it's important to say yes. Always to say yes.

Around the room, Kara tribal men, some in Western clothing and others wearing tribal skirts and jewelry, filled nearly every empty space. The invitation to spend time with them was an honor. They wanted to express that they were thankful for the things we were doing for their people, and the best way they knew to show appreciation was to share a meal and conversation.

Simi offered to translate, telling us we were free to ask anything we wanted about their culture and customs. Jessie and I exchanged glances. The fact was, we had lots of burning questions and were eager to learn as much as the men were willing to share.

"Are you sure?" I asked Simi, surprised at the openness of his offer.

"Yes," he insisted, gesturing with his hands toward some of the tribal elders sitting in chairs against the wall. "They are my relatives. They will tell you anything you want to know."

Jessie and I leaned forward. The popcorn passed in front of us again. We both took small handfuls, then offered a few morsels to our kids, who were sitting near us on the floor.

"We only know a little about mingi. Can you explain more?" Jessie inquired.

After a long reply from one of the older men—in a language that sounded throaty and deep, sort of like wild bird mating calls—Simi began to translate. "There are spirits that live in Kara land. They are good to us. They make the rain come and keep us safe. They make the plants grow from the ground, and they keep the wild animals away. We have to keep them happy. We have to do things that they tell us to do, or they will not help us; they will not protect us." Simi shifted his weight a bit as he continued to translate.

"We can only talk about this because we are not on Kara land now," Simi added, the air thick with tension.

"The spirits say a child who is mingi must be killed, or else the spirits will bring bad things to us. If we keep a mingi child, the spirits will kill our cattle, or they will kill our families. The spirits are powerful. Sometimes they send snakes to homes, killing a whole family in one night. We have to listen to them."

Simi stopped, then nodded at me, encouraging more questions.

"How long has it been like this?" I asked.

This time another man, whose face was leathery and deep black and whose eyes revealed decades of struggle, answered. "Mingi has always been part of our culture. The stories we hear from our ancestors tell about mingi and the children who had to be killed. About eighty years ago, the Kara people were very large. We were more than one hundred thousand people and ruled all the land in the area. But some people started to have a disagreement about mingi. Many families began asking questions about why we had to do this and why we could not keep our kids. After a while, it became a big problem, splitting our people into two groups: those who believed in mingi and those who did not."

The elder paused for a while, as if to reflect on the difficult days. Then, he started again. "A big meeting was held in Duss to talk about mingi. The elders talked for many days and finally made the decision that mingi would continue. We were not going to stop, because we were too afraid of what might happen. After that, more than half the Kara tribe decided to leave. They went farther south. We are not sure, but we think they are in Uganda now."

While the other men in the room listened intently, he continued: "Another time, about twenty-five years ago, the Kara people had a sickness. We call it sleeping sickness. If someone got the sickness and went to sleep, they died. Now the Kara people are only about three thousand. We have had a hard life."

As Simi interpreted, the elder nodded along, even though he didn't understand English. "We are thankful you are here to help our people," he added. "We love our children and do not want them to be killed. We are glad you are keeping them safe in Jinka."

Jessie and I sat stunned, unsure of what to ask next. We were trying to process the immense hardship these people had seen in their lives, trying to understand what it felt like to suffer for generations, living in terror of evil spirits.

I began to grasp that this was not just a superstition, like someone might have about walking under a ladder or breaking a mirror. No, this belief was very real to these people, a deep-seated fear that convinced them they didn't have a choice.

"Tell him we serve a God who is bigger," I blurted out in Simi's direction. "Tell him we know that God loves the Kara people, each and every one of them, and He doesn't want them to suffer like this."

As Simi translated those simple words of faith, the man nodded his head in agreement. In that moment, I knew we had to do more. Rescuing children was not enough. I was convinced that unless we brought the peace of the gospel, there'd be no stopping the practice of mingi. Without hope, the Kara would live in torment forever—living in anguish until they trusted a higher power, One who was greater than the spirits they feared.

My thoughts were interrupted by Jessie, whose motherly instincts drove home more questions. "What about the kids whose parents willingly gave them up in order to save their lives? Can those families ever be reunified?" she asked.

"Those children can never live in Kara," the man replied emphatically.

"But can they visit?" Jessie pressed in.

"They can come to visit, but they can never again sleep in Kara. The spirits will not allow them to do so."

†

We tucked our kids into bed, kissed them good night, and zipped up the tents we used as mosquito nets. Lying on our mattress, Jessie and I began to talk. "I didn't realize the fear was so real," Jessie said. "I knew it was an ancient tradition that they held onto, but I didn't realize they were in constant fear that these spirits would kill their families if they didn't do what the spirits said."

"I know," I agreed, resting my head on bended arm to look in her eyes. "But doesn't it make you feel there's a purpose for our being here—like we can actually do something to help these people?" I encouraged. "It just seems we're finally starting to understand how to help. It's not just about rescuing a few kids; it's the entire practice of mingi we need to help stop," I said.

"But isn't that too big for us to take on?" Jessie interjected.

Before I could answer, we were jolted to attention by shouts coming from our kids' room. Jessie and I darted toward the door, nearly knocking each other over in our hurry to see what was going on. Once inside we found our three children screaming in terror.

"What's going on?" Jessie called out, attempting to be heard over the yelling.

"There's a dog outside," Luella pleaded, her tiny figure shaking as she sat up in her tent, pointing toward the window. "He stood up like a man. His head was huge, and he was staring at me!" Jessie unzipped Luella's tent and climbed in to comfort her.

"I didn't see anything," Nickoli said. "I just heard Luella crying, and it made me scared, so I screamed too."

I gathered Ruth into my arms and climbed into Nickoli's tent to comfort them both.

"You have to go outside and chase it away," Luella insisted.

"There's nothing out there," I said, glancing out the window, trying to calm her fears. "It's just shadows, Luella. That's all—shadows."

"Levi, can you just go check?" Jessie encouraged, gesturing toward Luella, who was still shaking and crying hysterically.

"Okay," I said, rising to go outside for a look. Grabbing my flashlight, I walked into the pitch black, the tiny illumination barely piercing the darkness. I walked all the way around the house but saw nothing out of the ordinary.

When I returned to report that all was clear, my wife looked me in the eye. "I'm going to let her sleep in our bed," Jessie insisted as she clasped her arms tight around Luella. "She needs to be with us."

Once Luella was safe in our room, Jessie held her close, stroking her hair and singing softly into her ear, eventually rocking her to sleep.

"I think Luella heard too much today," Jessie whispered.

"I know. It *was* too much," I agreed, thinking back to the horrific details we'd heard together: snakes that killed families and children being drowned because their families were afraid of evil spirits. Clearly we hadn't done a good job of protecting our kids from what we were battling. Jessie and I agreed that from that moment on, we'd be more careful, no longer allowing our kids to hear things that would make them afraid.

"I can't stop thinking about what that man told us today," Jessie said. "How the children could never come back, that they would never be a part of their families again—that this is final. If education and reunification aren't options, then it makes me wonder if we should think more about getting these kids adopted into homes."

"I know," I said softly, careful not to wake Luella. "I've been thinking the same thing."

Jessie was right. We had to do something. We had to consider the future. Although we were doing our best for the kids, clothes and good food are not enough for any child.

"You know, there haven't been many new kids coming into the orphanage lately," Jessie went on. "I'm just saying, if there aren't going to be more kids coming in, then perhaps we should find adoptive families for the nine children we have now."

I knew in my gut Jessie was right, but I was keenly aware the adoption process wasn't going to be easy. Nothing was easy in Ethiopia, and I sensed this challenge was going to be monumental.

"Just look at the struggle we're having here: the water is hardly on, the food is scarce, and nothing ever seems to work," Jessie continued. "We'd be doing the kids a favor by giving them families, allowing them to live in a place where they could get a real meal three times a day and attend a good school."

It was at that point that Jessie and I became more determined than ever to give the children better lives. "These kids deserve a home, Levi," Jessie said. "Every one of them deserves a home."

†

We'd been in Ethiopia only a few weeks, but the slower pace of life and the passionate love with which the locals had welcomed us was starting to rub off on us. With each passing day I felt lighter. Even the kids were learning to greet each morning with newfound gratitude. We began to sit on the porch after the afternoon heat lifted, just to enjoy each other as a family, often joined by two or three of the orphanage children visiting our home.

One evening as we watched the kids playing a game of hide-and-seek, interrupted by loud giggling each time a child was found, I leaned over to Jessie and kissed her softly on the cheek.

The layers of warnings I'd heard back in America, "Your kids won't be able to handle it; you will ruin your family," were peeling away, revealing a wonderful picture underneath—one that as we sat with the cool breeze quietly brushing across our faces I wouldn't have traded for the world.

With my arm wrapped around the most wonderful woman I'd ever met and my eyes on our kids as they learned to love and interact with the children who only months before were sentenced to death, I wondered if this was our purpose. I let my mind wander back to the life we once lived—the one with offices, schools, parent-teacher conferences—and I knew we'd found our destiny.

6

WE SAT ON A FOAM MATTRESS on the living-room floor, reading books to our kids and talking about our new life in Ethiopia as candles flickered and cast moving shadows on the yellow walls. The power was out, and we had no TV anyway. We were enjoying just being together, learning to love anew.

Nickoli talked excitedly about the black-and-white lamb he and his sisters had discovered that morning, a short way up the road. They'd spied the frail newborn with part of a wet and sticky umbilical cord still hanging from its stomach. Wide-eyed, they'd watched the little critter stand up and stumble around, trying to gain its footing.

Immediately the lamb's mother came to protect her offspring from the kids, who by now had dropped to their knees, attempting to pet her baby. *Baaa*, the mother warned them as she bowed her head low, making a ramming gesture.

Even this baby has a mother to protect it, I thought to myself. *Even this one*.

While the kids played inside, Jessie and I moved to the porch to watch the blazing Ethiopian sun make its disappearance into the distant mountains.

"How can we go on?" Jessie asked, as she leaned in next to me. "How can we live here and not adopt at least one of these kids?" she almost begged, not really expecting me to have an answer.

I reached forward to grab my mug of tea. "But there are so many children," I countered, still unsure what she was getting at. "I mean, all we see every day are orphans— kids with no families, kids who need families."

The second those words came out of my mouth, I knew I was wrong. I sensed in my heart that someone had to start taking up the slack, that if everyone believed the kind of nonsense I'd just uttered, nothing would ever change.

Besides, it was clear whom Jessie was talking about: Edalawit. That little baby was burrowing her way into my wife's heart. And it was time I understood that.

"She's so small, so helpless, and the orphanage isn't really set up to take care of babies. All the other kids are so much older. She just gets left in the corner," Jessie said, the emotion rising inside her and her voice beginning to shake. "I don't know if we'd be allowed to adopt her, but I want to try."

As I looked into her eyes, I glimpsed Jessie's compassion for those in need. I couldn't help but remember her, so innocent and beautiful as she rounded the corner at the back of the church, elegant and stunning in her wedding dress of lace. I remembered our vows; our commitment to each other; our promise to stay creative, adventurous; our oath that once joined, we would become more together than we were apart.

I felt the fire of Jessie's passion flowing toward the mingi kids, and particularly to this baby, this tiny infant who had no mother.

Had it really been ten long years? Was it possible that it had taken this long to circle back to the commitment we'd made in that church converted from an abandoned grocery store? Never once had I wavered in my love for Jessie. Never once had I doubted my vows. But that night, as I watched tears stream down her face and felt her heart torn open, I asked myself a question: *Were we meant for something more, a higher purpose, a broader destiny?*

Of course, I knew the answer: We *were* made for more.

Meeting needs was our mission. Our passion. Not for personal gain. Not to find an identity in a cause. Not to experience life in a fuller way. It was our passion because we were thankful for what we had, thankful for a God who loved us, thankful for the blood in our veins and the fire in our hearts that compelled us toward our destiny.

Gazing out at the piercing sky, Jessie reached for my hand and whispered Edalawit's name.

And together, we dared to believe.

†

We spent the next few days in a dreamy state, talking nonstop about the possibility of bringing a new baby home. Jessie was head over heels in love with little Edalawit, and despite not being all that excited about starting over with diapers, especially considering our remote location, I was not hard to convince.

Meeting needs was our mission. Our passion. Not for personal gain. Not to find an identity in a cause. Not to experience life in a fuller way. It was our passion because we were thankful for what we had, thankful for a God who loved us, thankful for the blood in our veins and the fire in our hearts that compelled us toward our destiny.

We'd already worked through the theological implications of adoption. We believed firmly that our family was called to adopt, and what's one more child when you already have three? But although we joyfully talked about the possibility, I put off asking Simi.

We were just starting to form a new relationship, and I wasn't sure how he'd respond. The truth was, we were still very new to Ethiopia, and we didn't know the culture yet. Even so, we were falling for a tiny newborn and just had to do something.

An attempt to find out about the international adoption process on the Internet turned up empty, not because the information wasn't there, but because the connection was just too slow. When we finally found a site that looked as though it might have some good tips, the connection would fail or part of the page wouldn't load.

Then one afternoon while I held Edalawit, Simi motioned me over. "I have been watching the way you and Jessie look at her. I believe it is in your heart to adopt this baby."

"Yes," I replied nervously.

"I will see what I can do to make her part of your family," he said, smiling.

I nodded in agreement as hope rose in my heart.

†

With the small baby in my arms, Simi and I made our way across the tiny town of Jinka. Motorcycles rushed past, blowing dust in our direction. As people walked by, they pointed out the spectacle—a tribal baby carried by a strange foreigner.

"Mingi," someone shouted, while several villagers snickered. Word about our mission was getting out in Jinka, and by now, some had figured out this small baby was from our orphanage.

"Not mingi," I replied, smiling at the crowd. It was important to me that people understood we didn't view these children as cursed. We were hopeful that over time the stigma would change. However, the culture ran deep; even outside the tribal lands, citizens in Jinka knew about mingi and understood what it meant for the children's future. "Tell them she's a blessing," I said to Simi, gesturing toward the group, now walking with us down the road.

Simi uttered something in Amharic, one of seven languages he knew fluently. One of the older children fired back several quick phrases. The conversation continued for a few minutes.

"What are they saying?" I asked as the boy turned and headed down another street.

"They want to know why you are holding her, why your family lives here. They think you are strange for wanting to live in Jinka."

"Tell them," I replied, "that we believe God loves everyone the same."

"Of course." Simi smiled. "I already did."

†

We arrived at a dingy compound with several small cement buildings lining the outer rim. Each structure had a low elevation, and the splotchy, fluorescent-green shell looked as though it hadn't been painted for at least thirty years. Simi made his way past several doors, reading the small signs along the way and looking for the right room.

"Here," he said, as he turned and disappeared into a dim space. Inside, an elderly woman sitting at a small wooden desk greeted us.

"Salam nesh," I said when I shook her hand, proud to have used an Amharic greeting I'd only recently learned. Simi and the woman talked for several minutes while I moved respectfully to the back of the room and leaned against the wall, holding tight to Edalawit.

"Next room," Simi said as he walked quickly past me. I hurried to catch up to Simi, who had by now entered a different office and was already deep in conversation with a man sitting at another desk. For the next forty-five minutes we went from room to room, shaking hands with government officials, only to be ushered off to a new area where Simi repeated his request. Again.

Each time I asked if progress was being made, I was told to be quiet. "Just wait," Simi would say as he waved his hand defiantly in front of me. After what seemed like hours, he finally emerged from a room and beckoned me inside. "He wants to talk to you," Simi announced, gesturing for me to hurry.

As I entered the room, I found a short Ethiopian man sitting behind a desk littered with stacks of documents.

"Hello. Are you fine?" he asked with a thick accent, stretching his hand toward mine.

"I am fine. How are you?" I answered, shaking his

hand. The man looked at me quizzically, clearly having reached the end of his English vocabulary.

He motioned for us to take a seat, and Simi and I nervously sat down on two dusty wooden chairs. I cradled Edalawit while Simi explained my adoption request in Amharic. After several minutes of back-and-forth discussion, Simi looked at me and calmly spoke. "He wants to ask you a few questions. Do not worry," he assured me, "I will translate."

"Okay," I said, smiling at the official and trying to look confident.

"Why do you want to adopt this child?" he asked.

"Well, we respect the Kara people," I started in. "And we want to do whatever we can to help. This child was mingi and has no parents willing to provide for her. We want to give her a family." Simi translated as the man squinted his eyes in intense deliberation.

"Will you keep her as a slave?" Simi translated.

Startled, I jerked back in my chair—hard. "A slave? No. Not at all," I insisted. "Not a slave. We want to keep her safe and love her forever. We want to raise her as our own—to be part of our family."

Now it was the official's turn to look startled as he, too, jerked back in his seat. "Part of your family?" he called out, shaking his head suspiciously. "Then why did you pick a girl?" he pressed.

I paused for a moment, trying to find a way to reassure him that our motives were good. I understood that he had no frame of reference for my request. Although Ethiopia was fast becoming a popular place for international adoption, no children had been placed from this remote area. "We chose her because she seemed to have the most need. Her story is more clear—her parents tried to kill her immediately after birth, so it seems there's no way she'll ever be able to go safely back home."

"She will grow up and work for you, am I right?" the man continued, unable to grasp what I sought—the purpose for the adoption.

I tried again. "When we lived in America, we adopted once before," I said, attempting to give context to our request. "We have three children right now. Two were born from my wife, and the other one was adopted in America from a family that could not care for her. What we want is to adopt this baby as well," I said, gesturing to the small baby sleeping peacefully in my arms.

"As a daughter?" He leaned in to get a better look at Edalawit.

"Yes, of course, as a daughter," I replied. "Absolutely. As a daughter."

"Daughter?" he mumbled, leaning back in his chair.

As if on cue, little Edalawit awoke and began to squirm in my arms.

For the next few minutes, nobody said a word. At one point Simi flashed me a worried look, unsure of what to do next. Taking the hint from Simi, I remained silent.

Suddenly the official stood up. "Go, and come back

in thirty minutes," he said, using his English once again while pointing at the door.

"Thank you," I replied, unsure whether my response was appropriate or if something else might be going on.

Making our way to the road, Simi smiled. "I am sure it will be good. He is an honorable man," he said, breaking the silence as we crossed the street to a small café.

"Really?" I asked, afraid to get my hopes up. "Are you sure?"

"Yes," he reassured me. "He seems to like you. Everything will be fine."

We waited for thirty minutes to pass while enjoying strong black coffee. Neither of us spoke a word. Despite my best efforts, I couldn't think of anything to say that didn't seem absurd.

"Let's go back," Simi suddenly announced, as he checked his watch for the twentieth time since we had sat down.

We made our way back across the dusty road and into the government compound. Once inside, we went to the official's outer office, where we were greeted by a receptionist who handed us a small piece of paper. She and Simi exchanged a few words in Amharic; then Simi accepted the document, and we headed out toward the street once again. "We need to make a copy," Simi said, as he maneuvered up a side street.

Ten minutes later we returned with a single piece of paper. It was heavy card stock and was printed with little colorful balloons along the outer rim, the kind one might use for a birthday party invitation. On the paper were a few words: *EDALAWIT BENKERT—Father LEVI BENKERT—Mother JESSIE BENKERT. Born April 7th 2009. Place Kara, Duss.*

And that was it.

A part of me wondered how the process could be that simple. But we were in a small town in a very remote area, and a government official had created the record. I pushed down any doubts, trusting this was just how things were done in Jinka.

We made our way back to the office, and within a few moments, the chief signed the document and administered his official stamp. After paying a small processing fee, the equivalent of $3.15, I smiled broadly and held Edalawit tight, and together we headed home.

"Are you kidding?" Jessie asked as I came in the door, almost screaming with excitement. "Is she really ours?"

"Yes, it's for real." I beamed, holding up the piece of paper for everyone to see. "Edalawit's ours!"

†

It was two in the morning. I was staring at the wall and bouncing our new daughter on my lap, trying desperately to console her. We'd been in Ethiopia for only a month, and already we'd adopted a seven-week-old infant. Although we were joyous, our lives had been turned upside down. Everything we knew had changed. The joy I'd felt, the elation of being somewhere that our family could be used by God, had been replaced by a sense of weariness.

I bounced my knees in a slight vibrating movement, trying to lull Edalawit back to sleep. Since coming into our home, she hadn't slept for more than two hours in any one stretch. And at night she particularly seemed to come alive, often crying uncontrollably at the top of her lungs. In order to get some rest, Jessie and I took turns every other evening rocking her.

Of course we loved Edalawit, but we were having a hard time adjusting. It's difficult to switch gears—to go from three kids who sleep all night to four kids—with one who never seems to sleep at all. Yes, we had wanted to adopt her. We were committed, no matter what, to giving our new daughter the life and family she deserved, but—wow—the stress felt overwhelming at times.

I wondered whether perhaps we had moved too quickly. We had only a few cloth diapers, just a handful that had been donated from America. We had none of the comforts you would normally give a newborn: a swing, a soft blanket, nice clothes. I knew taking this baby into our home hadn't created the situation, but things still felt chaotic.

As I rocked Edalawit and stared into space, a shadow suddenly emerged from the hallway. Startled, I jolted from my daze. "What are you doing?" Jessie asked firmly as she swooped down and swiped the baby from my lap, rocking her gently back and forth. "She's been crying for ten minutes!"

"I'm sorry," I told her, realizing I'd been so lost in thought, I'd completely tuned out.

Jessie paused. "I know, Levi," she said, her voice softening. "It's just so much, isn't it?" She whispered, "I get it; I really do."

"What's so much?" I asked, already knowing what she meant but wanting to hear her say it out loud.

"This big family. This living in Africa. This trying to run an orphanage. It's all so much. We don't even have a proper bottle to give our beautiful new daughter." Jessie sat down beside me, the wooden couch creaking in protest under our combined weight. "How can we make things better?" she asked, tears streaming down her face, our innocent baby now cradled in her arms.

I understood what she meant. Each day emotions had raced through our bodies like a roller-coaster ride. One week we'd get a good grasp on our new life—enjoying Ethiopia in every way—and the next week we'd be in so deep, so painfully deep, that we felt there was no way a single glimpse of light could reach us on this side of the planet.

I was too numb to answer, knowing full well that Jessie was only expressing what we were both thinking. I put my arms around her, embracing the incredible child between us. I had no words, nothing to tell her that would make things better. We both knew we'd adopted this baby to give her a home, to do what we could to make her life better, but we had to admit, despite tremendous love, our lives were unraveling.

"We just need faith," Jessie said, trying to comfort us both at the same time. "We need to focus on our purpose. Our lives may be in disarray now, but this is not a vacation; we have to remember, we're here to rescue children."

She was right. Yes, we were struggling to find enough food to eat every day, but so were the tribal people. Yes, we were in desperate need of God—painfully aware of our need for Him each day—but so was each and every mother who'd been told to kill her child because of perceived threats from evil spirits.

We were learning that doing what was right and doing what came easily were two very different things. We were also learning to rely on each other on a new level. The trials were pushing us closer together, adding a new depth to our relationship.

†

The first glint of morning sun was making its way over the large mountain peak that overlooked Jinka. All across the small town, mothers were waking up early to get started on their daily chores. Smoke was beginning to gather above the houses as more and more families prepared for breakfast.

We were headed for a medical trip to Addis Ababa,

and a light rap on the gate let us know our driver had arrived. As we made our way through the narrow exit and out to the street by our house, I questioned whether I'd really made the right choice of vehicle. The white Toyota Land Cruiser parked on the dirt looked as if it had been through several wars—and not on the winning side. Its tires were nearly bald, and the body had almost as much rust as paint.

"Hello," a short man said, stretching his hand out to greet me.

"Hello," I replied, returning his warm smile.

"I am driver," he said, grinning from ear to ear.

"Wonderful," I told him, turning and heading back inside the house to retrieve my family. I loaded our bags onto the roof rack and placed a small foam mattress on the floor behind the backseat.

"How many?" the driver asked, puzzled by the extra room I was making in the rear of the vehicle.

"We have four kids, and we're picking up two more at the orphanage," I explained. From the confused look on his face, I could tell I'd spoken too much English. I tried to think of a way to explain in Amharic but came up blank, so I settled on holding up eight fingers.

"Wow!" he shouted, stepping back and rolling his eyes a little. "I call to owner," he continued, shaking his head in disbelief. "Owner no be happy."

I nodded in understanding, then went inside to get more bags. A few moments later we learned that the driver's boss decided he wanted additional money because of the number of people riding in the car. "Owner say he need extra," he explained, handing me the phone.

For the next several minutes we negotiated, eventually compromising on a slight increase in price. Although I disagreed in principle, I was learning that everything in Ethiopia comes with a fee when you are viewed as a rich foreigner. It's not that locals are trying to take advantage of people; it's just expected that anyone with the means to do so should pay extra. And despite the fact we were living on less than eight hundred dollars a month, provided by The Rock of Roseville, our family still had one of the highest incomes in the city.

Once everyone was situated in the vehicle, we headed toward the orphanage to pick up Kero and Genet. Because the tribes do not use calendars, we could only guess the children's ages. Kero was estimated to be five years of age, and Genet was assumed to be a year younger.

When we arrived, the girls were grinning from ear to ear. They'd rarely had the chance to ride in a vehicle of any sort and were more than happy to go on an adventure with our kids, who'd already become their best friends. Laughing with excitement, Kero and Genet quickly hopped in the back with Nickoli, Luella, and Ruth.

†

Despite the girls' initial enthusiasm, we weren't ten minutes outside Jinka when it became clear that we were in for an exhausting ride.

"Shintabit," Kero said emphatically, pointing out the window, gesturing that she needed to relieve herself. Within moments we pulled over and let her out of the car. Now, you'd think a girl who grew up in the tribes, outside in the elements her entire life, would have no problem going anywhere, but this territory was new, and she was frightened. Jessie struggled to reassure her that everything was going to be okay. After ten minutes of Jessie's encouragement and gestures, and eventually succumbing to bribes of candy, Kero found a small shrub that suited her just fine.

Happily, she headed back to her seat, but the peace didn't last long. Once we were back on the road, dust formed around the children's eyes and on their skin. "It's all over me!" Nickoli shouted as we continued to bump down the rocky dirt road at a pace hardly faster than a jogger on a brisk morning run. "I can't get it off me," he complained.

"It's red and pasty," Luella joined in, rubbing her face and getting the cakey substance all over her hands.

I climbed into the back of the car and quickly found the source: the door had no rubber seal, and the breach created a constant stream of dust that made its way into the vehicle. Shrugging my shoulders, I crawled forward and planted myself back in my seat, wondering how long this trip was going to take.

The previous trek had lasted more than eighteen hours. But this time we seemed to be crawling along at an incredibly slow pace. I rubbed my temples and prayed the journey to Addis Ababa would go smoothly, reminding myself of the importance of our trip.

Kero had a painful cavity in one of her teeth. There was a dentist in Jinka, but when we asked about his reputation and whether or not he could take care of her cavity, we were told, "Many people die after going to him." Apparently he didn't have anesthetic or a way to clean his instruments, so his patients often ended up with infections that led to death. Consequently, we thought it would be a good idea to head to the capital city, where Kero might get professional care.

Genet, on the other hand, had a bump forming on her neck. It had been growing larger each day and was now about the size of a golf ball. We thought it would be wise to have her medically evaluated as well.

The health issues that arose were entirely new to us—nothing, it seemed, was familiar or recognizable. We tried our best to treat illnesses on our own, but the truth was, we were in way over our heads. Our medical manual, *Where There Is No Doctor*, was becoming quite worn.

It was the children's medical needs that kept us

focused and moving forward, down every mile of hot, bumpy roads.

My thoughts were interrupted when Kero suddenly decided that every toy and object in the car, no matter who was playing with it, belonged to her and should be placed securely behind her for safekeeping. Jessie and I attempted to get something from her little stash, but she smacked at us in retaliation and screamed at the top of her lungs. After several tries, we made the call that it was best to leave her alone so that everyone could at least ride in peace.

Once we decided to give up the battle, even the driver seemed relieved. Yes, Kero was holding everything in the car—including the baby's bottle—captive, but there was no way we were willing to retrieve the items unless we absolutely had to if it meant enduring more of her high-pitched screams. At that point on this long drive into Addis Ababa, Kero ruled the world.

†

For the next few hours the kids sat quietly in the back-seat. While we soaked in the tranquility, Jessie tried to call it right there: "I think it's over, Levi. The worst of it—you know, the painful process of adjusting—I think it's finally over." She smiled at me and squeezed my out-stretched hand, eyeing me for confirmation.

"We're actually getting pretty good at this," she

continued, as we discussed the progress from our first weeks in Ethiopia. Emotionally we were adjusting well and finally getting over the culture shock. "It's starting to feel more like home," Jessie added, her words sounding somewhat strange to me.

In some ways she was right. I was amazed at how far we'd come. It seemed only a few weeks before that we were ready to get on a plane and head back to America with tails tucked between our legs. It's the sensation one gets the first few months living in Africa, the feeling of being so incredibly overwhelmed that it's hard to breathe. I had coined an expression for that feeling—*Africa slapped*—although every time I used the expression, Jessie would roll her eyes and accuse me of being crass.

Crass or not, I had to admit I'd never met anyone who'd moved to Ethiopia who didn't go through that phase. It's like a baptism in the fiery depth of your emotions, where everything inside that you hold tight—things you normally keep hidden and locked up in the inner closet of your soul—comes out. And there's nothing you can do to stop it.

†

At only thirty dollars a night, we were more than willing to fork over the extra cash to stay in one of the nicer local hotels. And by "nicer," I mean a hotel with a warm shower. The reality was, we were pretty much ready to take a shower no matter how much it cost. We still had another full day of driving ahead of us, and this was the least we could do for the kids, who were beginning to come unglued.

Once inside, we showed the girls to the bathroom and shut the door behind them. About five minutes later, Kero called out to Jessie. "Mama," she said quietly, as Jessie opened the door to find Kero trying to figure out the faucet in the sink and Genet squatting on the floor of the shower and using the drain as a toilet.

"Well, it's a good thing we got a room with a shower," I laughed, as Jessie shot me one of her give-me-a-break looks.

Once everyone was clean and dressed for bed, we all fell asleep, exhausted and praying for a better day tomorrow.

†

The next morning, Jessie and I loaded everyone back in the car and once again headed for the open road. We drove along as Edalawit wiggled on my lap; Kero screamed over her secret stash; Genet, Nickoli, Luella, and Ruth complained about the unfairness of it all; and Jessie tried her best to play peacemaker. By the time we pulled into Addis Ababa, I was ready to strap myself to the roof of the car just to find some peace and quiet.

We checked into another small hotel, the sun having set hours before, and attempted to figure out the best way to arrange everyone's bed so we could all get some sleep. Although the hotel was clean, we felt uncomfortable there. Maybe it was the cover of darkness, or the fact that we were in a neighborhood we'd never been to before. Whatever it was, we quickly locked the door, trying our best to get comfortable.

There was only one full-size bed in the room and a couch in the corner large enough for one child. The other five kids had to find places on the floor to crash. We had a few sleeping bags but not enough for each person, so a couple of the kids had to sleep on towels placed strategically on the floor.

Jessie and I felt conflicted. Back home in California, our situation would be viewed as child neglect—this many kids in one small hotel room, not enough blankets and pillows to go around, and not even enough floor space to walk across the room. Yet here, in this situation, Genet and Kero were getting access to much-needed medical care; and while our children were giving up physical comforts, they were also learning about the world. In addition, they were beginning to grasp valuable lessons about giving to others, something we were convinced was important for our kids to understand.

That night, like every night along the trip, Kero awoke around two thirty, screaming in a fit of terror. We held her tight and tried to wait it out. Jessie and I prayed for her to calm down, hoping she would find peace, hoping that God would give her a sense of tranquility that we could not seem to provide. We tried our best to soothe her, but despite our efforts, she still managed to wake everyone else in the room. We got so accustomed to the startling early morning wake-up call that we began serving snacks in the middle of the night. After several nights of Kero's screams, we were all desperate for sleep.

†

While we spent our nights trying to rest, we spent our days searching for doctors willing to examine the kids.

"She is only a child," one dentist chastised, refusing to even look inside Kero's mouth.

"Pain is good for her. She will not die," mocked another, who also denied her an exam.

Jessie and I began to wonder if we should have taken the children to Addis Ababa, if we should have bothered to buck the system and give them what we felt they really deserved. Yes, in America there was no way we could have ignored their medical conditions, but we were now more than one thousand dollars into this one trip—money we could not afford to spend, taken from an already depleted account—to provide some basic medical services that were clearly not normal in this country.

Finally we found a Chinese dentist who agreed to fill Kero's cavity, and a dermatologist who told us that Genet had a raging case of ringworm that had started affecting her lymph nodes. We were thankful to have the medical conditions taken care of, but we were keenly aware that we were more than a two-day drive from home and hadn't yet had a full night's sleep.

"What do you think it's like to have a breakdown?" I asked Jessie one morning, as we lay in the tiny hotel bed mentally getting ready to take on another day. "I mean, do you think it comes on all at once or happens slowly?" I continued, honestly wondering if I'd reached the point where I just might crack. "What do you think it feels like to go crazy?"

"I think," she said, "it feels a lot like this." She laughed an unsettling chuckle, then got up, turned on her heel, and headed toward the bathroom, the only place where it was possible to get a moment of peace. Jessie and I had an agreement: we took turns every day giving the other ten minutes in the bathroom. Alone. I observed Jessie go in, looked at my watch, and started the timer.

†

I made my way across Addis Ababa in a bright-blue taxi, which parked in front of the embassy—a tired-looking structure that resembled a shabby DMV building in America. At the gate, the attendant checked my identification and asked why I was there. "I want to get a passport for our newly adopted baby," I explained.

"Go ahead in," he said, through the thick glass security window as the door unlocked with a distinct click.

Handing over my phone and keys, I headed down the hall toward the staircase.

At the top of the landing I found myself in a room full of Ethiopian people who, I assumed, were seeking travel visas to the U.S. Several of them spoke English fluently, well enough to sound as if they had lived in the States all their lives. I wondered at this strange new world before me as I flipped through my paperwork. There was not much to it: one colorful balloon birth document, a copy of Jessie's and my marriage certificate, and our passports.

"What do you think it's like to have a break-down?" I asked Jessie one morning. "I mean, do you think it comes on all at once or happens slowly?" I continued, honestly wondering if I'd reached the point where I just might crack. "What do you think it feels like to go crazy?"

"I think," she said, "it feels a lot like this."

"Levi Benkert," the voice crackled over the loudspeaker. "Window number nine."

I made my way through the roomful of people and over to the corresponding booth.

"I have a few questions about getting a passport for a child my wife and I recently adopted," I said, leaning into the microphone and sliding the three small pieces of paper underneath the window. On the other side of the thick, plate-glass window stood an intense-looking American woman. Her facial expression told me I was not going to like what she was about to say.

"What's this?" she asked, squinting her eyes and

almost growling as she gestured to the thin stack of papers before her.

"The adoption's been completed already. We live in Jinka and handled it through the local administrator," I explained, my voice shaking, caught completely off guard by her tone.

"You did no such thing," she laughed, looking straight into my eyes. "This document isn't valid for international adoption," she scolded, sizing me up for more. "America doesn't allow for this kind of paperwork, and neither does the Ethiopian government. If you really want to adopt her, you should give that child back to the orphanage and go through the correct process. But the way things are now, this baby is absolutely not yours."

My knees shook, and I began to stutter. Words wouldn't form in my mouth long enough to compose a complete sentence. "Really? Really?" was the best I could muster.

I fumbled for the documents as she handed them back to me through the slot under the glass.

"Thank you," I said, caught by the strangeness of my own reply. My hands trembled as I made my way through the maze of security, back to the street, and into a cab, wondering how I could have been so naive as to think any adoption could be that simple—even in rural Jinka.

From the rear of the vehicle I gazed through the window at the local scenery: lots of children, small children, dirty, alone, crying—many with no parents in sight. *What are we going to do?* I thought to myself, fighting off the darkness looming around me. Then the realization settled in: I had left the embassy without any solid information, nothing of real substance. I knew less now than I had before I arrived, only that we were in trouble. Big trouble.

I decided right then and there that I was not going to tell Jessie. She was having a hard enough time processing the trip. I was convinced the news might be more than she could handle. To be honest, I was pretty sure it was more than I could handle as well.

But as soon as I walked through the door of the small hotel room and looked into Jessie's eyes as she sat on the bed, one child in her lap and several more jumping behind her, I knew there was no way I could keep any of this from her. "Jessie," I said in a hushed voice as I switched on the television to distract the kids with an Arabic cartoon and motioned her toward the corner of the room, "let's talk over here."

Jessie stared hard, trying to evaluate what I was about to say by the look on my face.

"They told me she's not ours," I blurted out. "They told me the adoption isn't legal."

Jessie began to cry. The kids remained glued to the TV. And I stood there feeling like an idiot.

Maybe the lady at the embassy was right. Maybe I was out of my element. Every tiny step forward, every victory we celebrated, seemed to be met with a giant blow that sent us backward—much further back than we'd progressed.

Our heads were swimming. Edalawit was our daughter. She was four months old, and we had been with her all but the first seven weeks of her life. She was ours. We knew that, and yet, legally . . . Our hearts just couldn't go there.

Jessie walked over to the small baby, picked her up, and kissed her on the forehead.

I wrapped my arms around my wife and held her close. "It's going to be okay," I lied. "Everything's going to be okay."

†

That night, while my family slept, I went to my laptop and, in desperation, shot off an e-mail about Edalawit to the American Embassy. Afterward I closed my laptop, asked God for a miracle, and then climbed into bed, where I tossed and turned the rest of the night. I wasn't sure when an answer might come, or even if there was an answer, but I knew one thing for certain: I had to try. While Jessie and I waited for a sign of hope, friends from The Rock of Roseville—Rich, Melissa, Joel, and Adrienne—arrived in Ethiopia. After spending a few days in Addis to collect supplies, we loaded the cars and headed out on the open road. Although we made slow progress on the way back to Jinka, we were thankful to have an extra vehicle to spread the kids around.

But even with the extra space, the girls were getting restless. They missed their own beds and their nannies. After the first full day on the road, they were a mess. For hours on end, Genet screamed uncontrollably, clinging to Melissa for comfort.

When we finally arrived in Jinka, unpacked our bags, and got the children settled, the adults gathered around for a serious talk. "Are we thinking enough about the kids' futures?" Melissa asked as we sat on the floor of the living room and shared peanut butter sandwiches on locally made white rolls. "I mean, is this really the best place for them to grow up? Or should we think about other options for some of the children?"

"We've thought about other options," Jessie said as she spread peanut butter on another roll. Jessie and I were big fans of adoption. Ruth had been adopted through the California foster care adoption program, and we'd already discussed at length the prospect of getting the orphanage children into permanent families.

When we made the decision to adopt little Edalawit, we'd hoped to be an example to those around us. "At first, Levi and I thought we might encourage local families to adopt," Jessie explained. "But we found out the Ethiopian culture isn't exactly open to the concept."

"What about international adoption?" Adrienne asked.

"We've thought about that, too, but it seems like a

long, complicated process," I said cautiously, not wanting to dig deep into the bad news we'd recently been given about Edalawit.

"What about you guys? Wasn't the adoption process easy for you?" Melissa asked.

Jessie glanced my way, then looked down. It wasn't that we didn't want to share. It was more that we hadn't yet processed the news ourselves. We were still in denial, not allowing ourselves to even think of giving up the child we had so quickly come to love.

"Well," I said, letting the words come slowly as I tried to make up my mind exactly how to proceed, "while we were in Addis, I was given disappointing news."

I stared off through the window at our children playing in the mud, each of them covered from head to toe in the sticky red substance. Then I looked down at the small baby on the blanket next to Jessie. Our baby. She was playing with her tiny hands and cooing at the dusty light fixture that hung from the ceiling—the one with cascading pieces of glass that swayed in the wind when the door opened. I wondered if we'd ever be able to call this child our own or if she'd only been entrusted to us for a season.

"We don't know much," I went on. "But it turns out the adoption papers we were given weren't official. For now, everything's up in the air."

The room got quiet. I didn't have the strength to say more.

Rich broke the silence. "What if we went back to America and started talking to adoption agencies?" he said, speaking from a corner of the room where he sat leaning against the wall, legs stretched out in front of him. "Other people do it all the time. Hardly a week goes by in the States that I don't hear about a family who has adopted a child from Ethiopia. Melissa and I are more than willing to run things from the American side. I realize you guys aren't able to get much done from here. It's hard enough for you to check your e-mail in Jinka. How could you ever research international adoptions?"

For the next few hours we dreamed of possibilities. Although we weren't sure how to begin, we all agreed on one thing: the kids deserved to be in families.

†

Endale was a kind little boy with a very old soul. Only three, he projected a depth far beyond his years. He'd often sit in Melissa's lap, looking deep into her eyes. We could all see what was happening—he was crawling his way into Melissa's heart.

"We need to talk," Rich said one evening, as we walked to town to try our luck with the Internet.

"Okay," I said, sensing what might be coming.

"I think my wife is falling in love," Rich blurted out. "You know that little boy Endale?"

"Yeah," I said, chuckling. Of course I knew Endale. By now we knew each of the children well, despite the fact that we still didn't speak the same language.

"Melissa and I would like to adopt him." Rich paused, letting the words hang for a while, as if to absorb the magnitude of them himself.

Rich and Melissa had been married for four years and had planned to wait to have children. They wanted to be a little older before they started a family, and until this point, they hadn't felt ready. Their plan was to have at least one biological child and then later adopt.

That was before they met Endale.

"So you guys are thinking about adopting first?" I asked, trying to tread lightly. Rich and I were fast becoming good friends. But the reality was, we lived half a world apart, and the few conversations we'd had over the phone were more about funding for the orphanage than emotions.

"Yeah. We realize there really is no difference between an adopted child and a birth child. And if we're going into this thinking there is, then perhaps we shouldn't adopt in the first place. So, since each child is the same, the order they arrive doesn't really matter."

Rich had a point. Jessie and I had learned from Ruth's adoption that there is no difference. You love each child and would never dream of preferring one over another, no matter how, or when, a child entered the family.

"I couldn't agree more," I said, smiling. "But we're

going to have to talk to Simi," I told him. Even though Rich understood Simi was in charge of the local organization, I wanted to make sure he realized we could never make a decision like this on our own.

"Melissa and I know you guys are having trouble with your adoption," Rich said, as he lightly touched my shoulder. "We're going to do everything we can from the States to help out. We see your adoption as a priority because Edalawit's already living with you. Levi, you can trust us to do whatever it takes to help you get her adoption finalized."

"Thanks, man," I said, with a deep sense of relief. I knew we'd never get this done without serious help and felt grateful for Rich and Melissa's support.

†

When we arrived at the Internet café, I sat down to check my e-mail. I quickly pulled on the monitor and was astonished to find it worked on the very first try. I was so excited to have a connection in Jinka that I nearly jumped from my seat. Rich looked at me, puzzled. "Just trust me; this is rare," I said as I focused my eyes on my in-box, searching for anything of interest.

As the months had worn on in Africa and I dropped off the radar of those back home, fewer and fewer e-mails came my way. My eyes rested on a message from my former business partner, Micah. "We'd still love to come and see you someday," he wrote. I smiled at the thought. Micah was a good friend, one who'd stayed by my side through everything.

I clicked back to the in-box to see what else had come in and read, "OFFICIAL REPLY: USCIS Adoption Questions." I clicked on the e-mail and held my breath as I read.

> Dear Mr. Benkert,
>
> This is in response to your e-mail dated July 17, 2009. . . .
>
> Please be advised that you may file for adoption on either form I-600A or I-600, depending on how far along you are on the adoption process. . . .
>
> The Consulate will forward your petition, fee receipt, valid copy of your Ethiopian residence visa and fingerprints to our office. . . .
>
> We hope that this information is helpful to you.
>
> Regards,
>
> USCIS
>
> United States Embassy
> P.O. Box 606 Village Market
> 00621 Nairobi, Kenya

I wanted to kiss the screen. I'd hardly expected a reply to the brief e-mail I'd sent late that evening in Addis after everyone was asleep in our cramped hotel room. Now I was discovering there was a chance! Sure, the adoption process might get complicated, but at least it was possible.

After I showed Rich the e-mail, he gently pointed out the message was not quite as exciting as I was making it out to be. But I just shook it off.

"You don't understand," I told him. "This is the first bit of good news we've had about Edalawit in months. At this point, I'll take any shred of hope I can get."

Rich smiled, and after he scooted into the rickety chair and checked his own e-mail, we headed back home.

As soon as we made our way through the rusty gate to our house, I took Jessie aside and told her about the message from the embassy. "It's not totally clear how it all works, but they did make adoption sound feasible," I said, happy to be finally sharing some good news about the baby we loved so much.

"So it's really possible?" Jessie asked, slowly letting herself open up to the belief that this time things might be for real.

"Yes!" I assured her. "It's totally possible!"

†

"I can't take it anymore!" Adrienne said as she pulled the rope from the deep hole, revealing another nearly empty bucket of muddy water. It had been eight days since we'd arrived in Jinka with our guests in tow, and not once had the water or electricity been on.

The rain had been light that year, and everyone in town was telling us the same things: their wells were running dry, and the town reservoir was totally empty. If it didn't rain soon, we were going to find ourselves in serious trouble.

While we tried to comfort Adrienne, Joel came through the gate carrying two heavy black grocery bags. "I found a shop that had some water," he shouted, looking as though he might just do a little dance right there in the dirt. "The shop owner charged me double, but at this point I don't really care," he said, grinning from ear to ear.

We all rushed forward to help him carry the bags. After placing the ten one-liter bottles on the kitchen table, we discussed how to ration them out. It was clear there wasn't enough water for showers. We had to be careful that we had enough to drink. We agreed that until we could find more, we'd each take one bottle to drink and leave the rest for cooking.

Over the next two days we did our best to conserve our water, while the supply faded fast. Then, just when we thought things couldn't get more desperate, the water came back on. At first it was only a trickle, but little by little it increased to full force, just in time for a quick celebration before our guests headed out of Jinka on their way back to America.

7

THE SWEET SCENT of bright red flowers cascading from the tree above us infused the night air. I shifted my weight on the wobbly plastic stool to keep it from collapsing and waited for Simi's answer.

I'd laid it out clearly, challenging Simi, pushing him to think about the children's futures, and asking him to consider moving into the orphanage so he and his wife, Weyto, could become full-time houseparents.

The bottom line was, I had no idea how Simi would respond.

I was beginning to ask the hard questions about the children's emotional well-being, but it was pretty clear that if anything was going to happen, it would have to be Simi and his wife who'd need to step up.

We'd been with the kids long enough to know they needed more than what they were receiving. We knew the children were going to grow up, and we needed to plan for their futures. The way things stood now, the orphanage felt more like day care than a home.

While Jessie and I loved the kids with all our hearts and were committed to seeing the orphanage through, we knew that if any of our own children got sick, we'd have to leave Ethiopia. We wanted to build something sustainable, and that meant Jessie and I could never be houseparents. That responsibility could be fulfilled only by a local.

I leaned back and let the words hang in the air, their intensity hovering like heavy fog. Finally, after a long pause, Simi opened up. He spoke of plans for his future: his political aspirations, his desire to attend school—plans that did not include living in Jinka long term.

I listened closely, sensing where he was headed but not wanting to help him along. If change was going to happen, it would have to be Simi's decision.

"I think we should look for adoptive families in America, so we can focus our attention on saving more children from death," he said thoughtfully.

"Are you sure?" I asked, afraid to be hopeful. Even though Simi had encouraged us to adopt Edalawit, I wasn't sure how he'd feel about more children placed in permanent homes.

"Yes, I am sure. But I have to be careful with my people. They might think I am profiting from the children. I have to go to them first to see if they agree. No matter what, Levi," he said, his eyes flashing with passion, "we can never make money from the adoptions."

I was thankful for Simi's integrity. I agreed whole-heartedly but was a bit confused nonetheless. I knew very little about the international adoption world and didn't quite understand what Simi meant by "making money." Were there people profiting from adoptions? Were some orphanages treating children as little more than commodities?

My focus went back to the orphanage. I mentioned a few ideas Jessie had, simple things to make the children's lives easier: toilet paper in the bathroom and more containers to hold water when the pipe ran dry.

Simi tried to take it all in, but he was extremely busy. In the months we'd been in Jinka, we'd spent only two weeks together. The rest of the time he spent traveling back and forth between the tribes and Addis Ababa, meeting with elders and government officials. Simi was one of the few educated men from his tribe and had far more responsibilities on his plate than the orphanage.

At times the chasm between the cultures felt too large to bridge. That evening, Jessie and I talked through the frustrations.

"I know it's hard," Jessie said, wrapping her fingers around my hand as I scratched at the knotty ripples in the roughly made wooden table in our living room. "But the kids are worth it. Many of them wouldn't be alive if someone hadn't been willing to step up. The frustrations are worth it. It's all worth it, Levi. All of it."

†

Ruth was sitting in a chair, swinging her feet playfully. I was attempting to put on her shoes when the phone rang. Patting her leg gently, I smiled, reached over to the table, and picked up the receiver.

It was Simi. He'd been gone for more than a week, and I had no idea when he would return. Seeing his number pop up on my phone made my heart skip a beat.

"I can only talk for a moment, but I must tell you the news," he said with excitement. "I spoke with the local orphanage board and tribal elders who are in Jinka for a meeting. All of them agreed; we can begin the adoption process."

I felt exhilarated. This was huge.

Simi apologized for the quick call, promising to share more soon. After a hasty good-bye I walked back to Ruth, who was waiting patiently in the chair, finished tying her shoes, and gave her a hug. I smiled when I recalled her stateside adoption. We were a happy family. Adoption had worked for us. I wondered if it was too much to hope that all the children in the orphanage could be so fortunate.

†

A few days later, Rich and Melissa called from California. When I told them the news, they were ecstatic. "We'll start making inquiries to find the best adoption agencies in Ethiopia," Rich said. "I'm sure there are some good ones we can work with."

Within days, Rich and Melissa came through. They'd found an agency that looked promising, one with a long track record and a good reputation with the American Embassy. But although we tried and tried to reach their office in Addis Ababa, the phone connection wouldn't cooperate. Every time we managed to speak to a staff member, they'd need another document from us—something that was nearly impossible to deliver over the weak Internet and fax lines.

Jessie and I finally came to the conclusion that we'd have to make another trip to Addis if we were ever going to get things rolling.

†

I booked a Land Cruiser, and together our family made the long journey north. Saying good-bye to everyone at the orphanage was harder than we had anticipated. We knew we were leaving for only a couple of weeks, but tears flowed all around as we tried to assure our new friends that the trip was only temporary.

We were hopeful we'd see some progress with the orphanage adoptions, as well as with Edalawit's. We needed to get some closure for our family, too. Jessie and I were desperate to get our family out of limbo.

The trip to Addis went smoothly. Our family was

adapting well to a nomadic lifestyle. And we were learning some tricks to make the trip easier. Our two-year-old, Ruth, was allowed to watch as many shows on the iPod as she wanted. It was better than forcing her to stare out the window for hours. Better for all of us.

Once in Addis, we met up with Yabi—the cabdriver who'd helped set up the orphanage. Over time we had learned to rely on him. Yabi was an honest man with a heart to help the people of the south, and his compassion for children was something we hadn't experienced anywhere else in Ethiopia.

He'd arranged to rent a small apartment from a friend, where we could stay for two weeks. The apartment had two bedrooms—each the size of a mattress—and a tiny kitchen and living room. For the next couple of weeks, we'd call this our home.

Every day while I attended meetings with adoption agencies and embassy staffers, I'd leave Jessie and the kids behind. And every night when I returned, my entire family was jumping out of their skins.

"We're going crazy here," my wife would tell me. "The kids are bouncing off the walls, and there's no place to take them," Jessie would say, pointing to the small parking lot outside the apartment, full of trash and animal droppings.

I tried desperately to move the process forward, to make some sort of headway, but despite my best efforts, I came up short. Hardly anyone had answers, and the few who did gave me the creeps. One guy appeared to want to sell the kids. "Just drop them off at my orphanage, and I will draw up the papers," he told me impatiently.

When I asked him more about the process and explained that we already had families in America interested in adopting the children, he quickly stood up and walked away.

"It's not worth my time," he said, waving his hand dismissively.

Something about the way the children in his orphanage were cared for and the way he so quickly dismissed me when I tried to stay involved with the process bothered me. I was never able to put my finger on what it was exactly, but a few weeks later an American family who'd been through the adoption process with this man's agency filled us in. "They're selling children," the husband and wife told us when we sat down together over coffee. "All the paperwork we got was a lie. Not a single bit of it was true, and yet by the time we arrived here, it was too late. What could we do—send this child out on the streets?"

Jessie and I were seeing more and more that the world of international adoption was full of dark and scary characters. Things were not always as they seemed. I took heed of the sick feeling in my gut and did as much research as I could on every agency.

But despite my efforts, each step I took revealed two more to go. I quickly learned the ugly side of what should be a wonderful experience. Jessie and I believed passionately in adoption. But each day as I dug deeper and deeper into the international process, I found corruption and money-hungry brokers. The reality of the situation tore me apart. *How,* I wondered, *could something so beautiful be overcome by so much darkness?*

†

A few days before our return trip to Jinka, I met someone I could trust—the man Rich and Melissa had recommended. The director of an international adoption agency, he'd been out of town for a while and had just arrived back in Addis.

Jessie and I believed passionately in adoption. But each day as I dug deeper and deeper into the international process, I found corruption and money-hungry brokers. The reality of the situation tore me apart. How, *I wondered, could something so beautiful be overcome by so much darkness?*

"We can help you navigate through the legal process for the orphanage children, including Edalawit," he told me reassuringly.

This man had more than thirty years' experience and was well known as the foremost authority on Ethiopian adoptions. He shared openly about the corruption problems and clearly defined his organization's policy. "We never participate in such activities," he said, "not under any circumstances."

Through many other sources in town, we were thankful to be able to corroborate the reassuring feeling we got while meeting with him. The director and the agency he headed had a flawless reputation with both the Ethiopian government and the American Embassy.

He explained the long road ahead, all the government agencies we'd be required to work with, and the various letters we'd need signed for each one of the children. It was clear that if we were going to go this route, our family would have to live in Addis Ababa. There was no way the process was going to go forward unless we applied ourselves full time to making it happen.

We'd done as much research as possible, followed every trail we could on the adoption process, and come to the clear conclusion that this organization would be the best one for us. In fact, by the time we made that decision, no other agency was left on our list. Out of more than seventy agencies working in the country, only one of them had the reputation and the credibility we felt we could trust.

†

While we waited outside the airport arrival gate, watching intently for a familiar face, our kids ran circles around our feet. "Are they here yet?" Luella repeated over and over, her face bright with anticipation.

"Not yet," Jessie said, smiling, "but soon."

And then we saw them—weary from the long plane ride but overjoyed to have finally arrived: Jessie's mother and sister, Alison and Donia.

The kids jumped up and down, and all the adults cried. We hugged until our arms were sore, then practically danced through the airport in search of their luggage. We found their bags in record time and made a dash toward the parking lot—excited to take our guests back to Jinka to share our new world.

The ride was long, but our newfound joy at having family with us kept us going. The children were thrilled to see their grandmother and aunt, and Jessie was beside herself with happiness. For Jessie and me, the trip was bittersweet. We knew that for now, this would be the end of living in Jinka full time. We hoped that eventually we'd move back south, but we'd learned enough about the adoption process to know we'd need to be in the north for quite a while to get everything rolling.

Our plan was to be in Jinka just two weeks and then return to Addis once again. We contemplated how to break the news to the orphanage staff. We were sure that, like Jessie and me, they'd be sad. But we were also certain that this was how it had to be if we were going to get anywhere with the adoption process.

When we arrived home, things weren't quite as we'd hoped. The water and electricity were off. Again. Only this time, Jessie and I were ready. Over the past several months we had learned that if we set out buckets, we could collect enough rainwater for our needs. And, thankfully, Alison and Donia were troopers. They handled the frustrations of life in rural Ethiopia well and never complained. Not even once.

Neither Jessie's mother nor her sister had done much traveling. Outside of Mexico, this was their first trip abroad. I was keenly aware of the potential for disaster. We had seen many travelers fall into a state of emotional disarray within just a few days of landing in Ethiopia. But to my surprise, Alison and Donia seemed to be doing fine.

During the excruciatingly long car ride, their spirits remained high. Even after arriving in Jinka, Alison and Donia took things in stride. I wondered if they were just stuffing their emotions, because after all, this was the place where Jessie and her family had chosen to live.

One afternoon as we sat around a tiny wooden table, I attempted to find out what they were really feeling. "So, what do you think?" I asked, hoping to get a straight answer out of either one of them.

"It's wonderful," Alison assured me with a smile.

"Really?" I asked, trying to make her feel comfortable enough to lay it on the line. Perhaps I feared that sooner or later my mother-in-law was going to tell me how crazy I was for doing this to my family. Her family. If there were bad feelings, I wanted to get them out on the table.

"It's not bad," she continued cautiously.

I leaned back in my chair and braced myself for what I anticipated was coming.

"It's not where I'd choose to live, but after seeing what good you've been able to do here, I can see how you felt you needed to move to Ethiopia," she said.

"So you don't think we're crazy?" I asked, letting out a deep sigh of relief.

"Not at all," she said with growing confidence. "It's really a beautiful place, and the kids are getting an experience they'll never forget. Besides, this is where God called you. How could I say you're crazy for following your calling?"

Within a couple of days Alison and Donia got so comfortable with their new surroundings that they made us an offer we couldn't refuse: they would sit with our four kids for the evening so Jessie and I could get away for a long-overdue date night—something we'd rarely had the opportunity to enjoy.

It was obvious from our quick response that we didn't need much coaxing. We jumped at the chance, kissing our kids good night as they snuggled on pillows near their grandma and aunt, surrounded by a pile of their favorite books.

As we walked away from our compound, hands clasped tightly, Jessie and I smiled at each other. This was the first time we'd been away from the kids since we arrived in Ethiopia, and we felt free. As we made our way across town, our steps were light.

Jessie and I spent the evening eating Injera at a small local restaurant and talking excitedly about our Ethiopian adventures. As we shared the spicy food, smiling and laughing together, I realized how thankful I was for my wife. Without a doubt Jessie was rising to the challenge of life in a remote village, and I was impressed. Money was tight, but our lives were full.

Jessie leaned in over the large plate of food and smiled warmly. "Did you ever think we'd be living in a place like this?" she asked.

I shook my head in disbelief. "Honestly, I never would have imagined it in a thousand years."

I looked across the table at the most beautiful person I'd ever seen. Jessie was thriving; she was glowing in a way I'd never seen before. I closed my eyes and tried to burn an image of Jessie into my mind—as she was now, in this moment—so I could remember it forever.

†

For two weeks we did our best to show Alison and Donia around Jinka. We took hikes into the mountains and walked along the river that wound its way through town. But we spent most of our time at the orphanage.

They quickly acclimated to the pace of things in the deep south, learning the names of the children and discovering why we loved living in Ethiopia.

The water and electricity stayed out the entire time they were with us. Jessie and I joked that the water always seemed to shut down when we had guests, making them feel sorry for us and the life we'd chosen. We did our best to adapt, setting out buckets to catch rainwater and using as little water for showers as possible. If we had learned one thing living in Ethiopia, it was that it's not all that hard to take a shower with a one-liter bottle of water. You just have to be very careful—when showering by the liter, timing is everything.

†

Alison and Donia kept the kids busy while Jessie and I once again packed our belongings into duffel bags and suitcases. Moving, it seemed, had become our new normal.

We were optimistic that our life in the big city—one that was sure to involve tons of paperwork and government meetings—would be rewarding. As had become our tradition, we hoped for the best, said a prayer, and then jumped in headfirst.

If we had learned one thing living in Ethiopia, it was that it's not all that hard to take a shower with a one-liter bottle of water. You just have to be very careful—when showering by the liter, timing is everything.

Besides, it had to be done. Moving to Addis was a necessary part of the adoption process. By now the ten kids at the orphanage were like family, and we desperately wanted them to have new mothers and fathers of their own. If it had been possible, we would have adopted them all ourselves.

So we piled our stuff on top of an old Land Cruiser and took off on the rugged road toward the north. Our children had grown familiar with the endless twists and turns and had found creative ways to entertain themselves: songs, stories, a word game. Life was simple. And it was good.

†

After a week in an Addis hotel we found a tiny house to rent in the center of town. It had a small, grassy yard—a far cry from the open spaces and rolling mountains we'd left in the south, but with enough room for the kids to play. And there were dairy products in Addis, including a small ice-cream shop, where our children savored every bite with glee.

And then it was over. Alison and Donia's monthlong visit had come to an end. Jessie and I helped them pack while the children slipped little mementos into their bags: a drawing, a note, a wilted flower.

The trip to the airport was difficult, and the goodbye hugs heartbreaking. Although everyone tried to be strong, tears flowed freely. Yet in the midst of our sorrow, there was a quiet assurance, a powerful sense that Alison and Donia's visit had been a sacred gift—one our family would never forget.

8

FROM THE MOMENT Chowki had discovered she was pregnant, she knew her baby would be killed. Once she had given birth to little Abreham, her husband, the elders, and the neighbors all agreed: "You should stop breastfeeding and let him die," they insisted.

But Chowki refused.

Fearful of the mingi curse, Chowki's husband told her that if she wanted to keep the baby, she'd have to leave their home.

So when Abreham was four months old, Chowki moved into the orphanage with her baby. She knew that one day she'd have to return to her village and leave Abreham behind, but she loved her son and wasn't ready to let him go.

From time to time her husband would visit. "You need to leave the baby and come home," he'd tell her.

"No. He is my son," she would always insist.

"He is mingi," her husband would flatly reply. "You need to come home and have another child with me."

Chowki was her husband's second wife. At times we wondered whether her refusal might be an excuse to get away from an abusive home. We prayed with Chowki, telling her we'd support her no matter what she decided and that we'd care for Abreham if she felt she needed to return to her village.

The pain in Chowki's eyes was ever present. When she ate, she would stare off into the distance. When she washed clothes, her eyes would tear up as she choked down the pain.

Of all the children at the orphanage, Abreham was the only one living with family. So we were able to see up close Chowki's example of a mother's love for her mingi child. And it burned.

The practice of mingi tore at the tribal people. We continued to search for solutions, but nothing seemed to work. We offered to purchase a small home in Jinka where Chowki could live and raise her son, but her husband stepped in and refused to allow the plans to move forward. We even invited him to come and live with her, but he refused.

One afternoon Chowki's husband showed up at the orphanage with an announcement. "In a month I am coming back to get my wife," he declared. "Then she will leave with me." If there is one thing we knew about the tribal culture, it's that a wife obeys her husband when he gives her an order. And this was a very clear directive.

In preparation, over the coming weeks Chowki tried her best to detach from her son. She pushed him away and instructed the nannies to treat him just like the other children. At first it worked. When Abreham approached her, she'd push him away. But when he started to show interest in the other nannies and Chowki could handle it no more, she'd pull him back in. Then, remembering her husband's words, she'd push him away and start the process all over again.

One afternoon Chowki's husband showed up at the orphanage with an announcement. "In a month I am coming back to get my wife," he declared. "Then she will leave with me." If there is one thing we knew about the tribal culture, it's that a wife obeys her husband when he gives her an order. And this was a very clear directive.

Shortly after we moved to Addis, we got word that Chowki's husband had arrived to take her home, leaving Abreham alone at the orphanage. Chowki had said goodbye to her son for the last time and headed toward her grass hut in the village.

†

Over the next few months our family settled into our new home while I spent every moment I could working on adoption paperwork. Before we knew it, the holidays were upon us.

It was the week before Christmas, and Jessie and the kids were feeling homesick.

With a mug of steaming coffee in my hand, I searched the Internet and dreamt of sending my family on a surprise trip to America. Edalawit and I would have to stay behind this time, until her adoption was complete. I cringed when I saw the price of tickets, especially during the holidays. Getting four people halfway across the world was no small task.

On a whim I shot off an e-mail to Rich and mentioned my idea.

A few moments later my phone rang. I looked at the number. It was Rich. Could he possibly be calling that quickly about the message I'd just written? Just in case, I walked outside to talk. "Hey," I said.

"Hey," Rich repeated excitedly. "So your family needs a little rest time?"

"Yeah, Jessie and the kids are getting pretty lonely, and I had this crazy idea I might be able to get them home for a little break. It's probably a bad idea, though," I said, aware by now that there was no way we could pay for the trip. In fact, at this point I was feeling pretty stupid that I'd even sent the idea to my friend, knowing he wasn't in a position to help.

"Tell you what, man," Rich said. "I'm going to make some calls around the church to see if we can find a few people willing to help. I think it's important your family take a break when they need one. The last thing we want is for you guys to burn out."

I was stunned. "Are you kidding?" I asked.

"I'm serious. Let me see if I can find some folks who can pitch in."

We talked for a few more minutes about the adoption process—the frustrations I was experiencing and the hope we held for the future. By now, Rich and Melissa had made up their minds to adopt Endale and were getting their paperwork lined up.

"I'll get back to you soon and let you know if I can find enough people to pull this off," Rich said, before saying good-bye.

I decided it was best not to mention anything to my family. Not yet, anyway. I didn't want to get their hopes up until I was sure things were a go.

But when I checked my e-mail just a few hours later, there was a message from Rich:

> Okay, we made some calls, and we're going to make this thing happen, Levi. Go ahead and book the flights for Jessie and the kids!

I shot back a quick thank-you and shouted the news to my wife. Ten minutes later I was in a taxi on my way to buy tickets. I knew if I acted quickly, I'd be able to get my family back home—just in time for Christmas Eve.

†

Jessie, Nickoli, Luella, and Ruth had been gone for a week. I was lonely and missed them desperately, but I was enjoying the one-on-one time with little Edalawit. And I had just heard from Simi: "I just got a text from Simi and am so excited," I wrote in my blog. "My hands are shaking as I write this. Simi says that we rescued two more kids! That is literally all I know at this point because he is out of range and although he was able to send a text to me, he does not seem to be getting mine. I will let you know when I know more."

Later that evening my phone rang. It was Simi, excited to share more details about the dramatic rescue. The two boys were from the Bena tribe and had been left for dead. The smaller child had been denied food and water.

"He almost died," Simi said. "His family tried to kill him by refusing even basic sustenance."

"Is he sick?" I pressed, on hearing the news of his struggle.

"I believe he will be fine," Simi said.

"Really, Simi," I insisted, "if you want me to send a car down to take him to the hospital, I can do it."

The connection dropped. I was feeling conflicted, wondering if I should do more. Then I remembered Preston and Eric, two young guys from California who were volunteering for a few months at the orphanage.

I quickly dialed their number, and after a couple of rings, Eric answered.

"Simi's in the car on the way back from the tribes," I said, jumping right in. "One of the kids sounds like he might be very sick. Do you think you guys can meet him at the orphanage and check him out?" I was almost begging.

"No problem," Eric told me. "We'll be happy to help."

While I waited to hear back from Eric, I tried to keep busy—doing more paperwork, washing dishes, even pacing the floor—but nothing I did provided the distraction I sought. After a few hours I tried calling again but received an error message telling me the network was down. I redialed every few minutes, but to no avail.

Finally at around eleven I went to bed. Unable to find out more and frustrated that I was so far from what was happening, I tossed and turned all night.

When morning came, I dialed the number again. This time the call went through, and Eric answered.

"I think you should get down here right away," he said. "Something's really wrong with the older boy."

"What is it?" I asked, fearful of his answer.

"I don't know," Eric told me. "It's something really bad. I can hardly look."

"What do you mean?" I pleaded.

"It's his rear. It's turned inside out, and something is sticking out about four inches," he said, sounding as if he might throw up.

"What?" I asked, unable to process what I was hearing.

"Yeah, it's pretty bad. . . ." Eric's voice trailed off. "And the other baby isn't doing well either. He's just lying here limp, with no expression on his face at all."

My mind raced. "I'll call you right back," I said, hanging up the phone and scrambling for the number for Captain Solomon, a kindhearted Ethiopian man who owned a small plane in Addis Ababa and had been trained years before by a missionary flight program. Through his business the captain often saves lives, and that's what he loves most about his work. He had once told me that if we ever had an emergency, I could call him for help.

I dialed his number, and he answered right away. The entire story flew out of my mouth in seconds: two rescues, two sick children, could he possibly help?

Yes, he would gladly assist. "I can leave in two hours," he said.

I scrambled for a way to make it all work. The flight was not going to be cheap, even though a discount was offered for medical emergencies. I called some friends and asked if they could take Edalawit for the afternoon.

After making my way to the airport with a small bag of formula and some medical supplies, I boarded the tiny plane. Within minutes we'd lifted off, heading through the clouds toward two very sick children.

My heart was pounding as I watched the beautiful green landscape spread out beneath us. My stomach churned. I wasn't sure if it was the jerking motion of the tiny plane as it bounced through the air or my fear taunting me that

I'd just spent nearly all the money we had to care for the orphans on one forty-five-minute flight.

†

The plane hit the ground with a jolt and then bounced back into the air. I gripped the handle in front of me and winced, hoping the rough landing would end safely. Finally we came to a complete stop, and I saw Preston and Eric in the distance, each holding a child and each in a state of panic.

"What's going on?" I shouted as I jumped out of the small door on the side of the plane.

"These kids are pretty sick." Preston almost cried. "The older one is doing a bit better. But this little guy is not hanging in well at all."

I glanced at little Teraffe, and right away I knew something was terribly wrong. His skin seemed to hang off his body like a leathery appendage. His eyes were rolled back in his head, and he looked as though he might not have much life left.

My stomach churned. I wasn't sure if it was the jerking motion of the tiny plane as it bounced through the air or my fear taunting me that I'd just spent nearly all the money we had to care for the orphans on one forty-five-minute flight.

Within ten minutes of landing we had reboarded the plane. Eric held on to Hesak, the older of the two children, and I held tight to Teraffe as we headed into the sky once again. The noise in the plane was too loud for conversation. Eric and I tried to talk for a few moments but gave up when we realized we'd have to yell to hear a word.

Unable to communicate, I focused on the small baby in my arms. I couldn't really determine how old he was. He had several molars in his mouth, but he was only about the size of a five- or six-month-old. His eyes were sunken, and he did not open them once the entire trip.

I felt a desperate need for Jessie. *She would know what to do*, I thought. Jessie always knew what to do.

Holding Teraffe close, I prayed, "Lord, please have mercy on this little baby boy." For a moment I imagined what it would be like if he didn't make it. I shuddered at the thought. I decided right then and there that this boy had to live. There was just no other option.

9

HESAK PROVED TO BE A SPIRITED CHILD. In the short period since we met, he had bitten me several times and thrown a Coke bottle at my head. Of all the children who'd come to the orphanage, he was the first to show anger and resentment. He distrusted everyone. I struggled to get my arms around him, to offer assurance that he was safe.

Once we reached the hospital, Hesak was given medication for the worms that had made his colon so unstable it had turned inside out. But Teraffe was not doing nearly as well. The hospital staff admitted him right away. His veins had almost completely collapsed, and the nurses had already spent hours trying to start and maintain an IV.

The next day, a visiting French doctor gave her report. "He's starting to show signs of improvement, but we were close to losing him last night," she said, in near-perfect English. "I'm sure if you did not bring him here yesterday, he would have died."

†

The adoption process was sapping our energy, and yet not one child had made it through the red tape. In the meantime, the orphanage had more than doubled in size. It had been two months since we'd been to Jinka, and there were now twelve additional children we hadn't met. It was time to return.

By now, the roads to southern Ethiopia felt like familiar friends—sort of like when you know a little too much about someone else's problems but you enjoy being around that person anyway.

While in America, Jessie was given a few media players by a wonderful family who wanted to help out. Their gift made the long trip more bearable. Each of the kids was able to watch shows and listen to music instead of staring out the windows for hours on end. The selection was limited, but the kids enjoyed having something to watch. While Ruth played *Dora the Explorer* on the infinite repeat cycle, Jessie and I were thankful for the headphones that allowed us to enjoy peace and quiet.

The moment we arrived and walked through the front gate to the orphanage, we were mobbed by children. We tried our best to learn every child's name, even asking the staff the meaning behind each one. We were told that Kotsa, the name of one sweet little boy, meant, of all things, "I have an itch." Hoping there had been a breakdown in communication somewhere along the line, we asked a few more staff to translate his name into their tribal language. But no, there was no problem with the translation; "I have an itch" was simply his name.

Jessie and I looked at each other.

"Mingi?" Jessie questioned quietly as we wondered whether perhaps children who were thought to be cursed were given less desirable names because the families knew their fate.

"Are you sure?" We were still hoping there was something we were missing. "How about this one?" we asked, pointing to Musse.

"It's like Moses in the Bible," they told us.

"Oh," Jessie said, thankful to have a name association that seemed positive.

"Got it—'Musse,'" I repeated.

†

Once we'd met all the new kids, Jessie and I had time to focus on the orphanage. And what we found was unsettling. The children were sleeping two, and sometimes three, to a bed. Meal quality had dropped dramatically, and the toilet and kitchen areas were a mess. The entire place smelled, and flies were everywhere. Jessie and I looked at each other warily. Something had to be done— and fast.

On one hand, the organization was saving lives, and our family was moving toward placing the children in adoptive families. Jinka was only a small blip on the map in one of the world's poorest countries, and that provided an interesting dilemma. The local staff were primarily uneducated, and those who were educated had not received basic hygiene training, nor did they understand most of what we asked them to do.

When we requested that the staff wash clothes in hot water to help keep the ringworm at bay, they thought we were just trying to give them more work. The reasoning behind our requests just wasn't getting through, no matter how hard we tried.

To address some of the issues, we found a small house to rent just a few blocks up the street and bought beds for the older kids. They would still go back to the main house during the day, but at least now we wouldn't have more than one child sleeping in a bed. And because of rising food costs, we more than doubled our grocery budget and added separate line items for cleaning supplies and cooking utensils.

We appreciated every one of the local staff, and we did respect their culture. In fact, it often seemed that we had more to learn from them about community and friendship than they did from us. But we were raising money in America to provide for the kids and felt accountable to provide the highest standard of care possible with the resources given.

†

As we spent more time in Jinka, our entire family was worn emotionally thin. We were feeling as if we might collapse under the pressure. On occasion, Jessie and I discussed what would happen if we left Ethiopia. "How could we?" we'd ask each other, knowing the care of the children rested firmly on our shoulders.

We were beginning to feel we were riding a roller coaster. Any hill we climbed, anything we accomplished, was sure to be followed by a fast descent toward the ground.

Although there were people helping stateside, we knew full well that the moment we left Ethiopia, everything would fall apart. Jessie and I were beginning to feel that we were the ones who needed rescuing.

We appreciated every one of the local staff, and we did respect their culture. In fact, it often seemed that we had more to learn from them about community and friendship than they did from us. But we were raising money in America to provide for the kids and felt accountable to provide the highest standard of care possible with the resources given.

†

Once the mosquito tents were set up and all the children were in bed, Jessie opened up. "Do you think we can actually make the changes happen?" she asked me, a troubled expression on her face.

"I think we have a lot of work ahead of us," I replied.

"But it feels so hopeless." Jessie paused before continuing. "I mean, if we're in Jinka, nothing seems to move forward with the adoptions. But when we're away in Addis, things at the orphanage fall apart."

"Maybe adoption isn't the best choice for these kids," I said, wondering if I was wrong as soon as the words left my mouth.

"What do you mean?" Jessie asked, studying my face for clues.

"I don't know, but it feels like we're spending all our time on paperwork and we're not keeping up with the kids. I wonder if we should just finish these few adoptions and focus on building an orphanage in Jinka for the rest of the children—a good one, like a village of small houses where they can grow up."

I stopped and waited for Jessie, not really knowing how she'd feel about my idea. The fact was, we were forging into new territory. We'd never had to think through this kind of thing before. We knew from our experience with Ruth that we believed in adoption. We were passionate about encouraging as many people as we could to adopt, but as we stepped back and looked at the numbers, at how much adoption was really helping in Ethiopia, we had to question whether it was the best solution.

Ethiopia has enormous orphan-care needs. The number of adoptions pales in comparison to the number of children needing families. If we or any other organization were going to do something, really make a dent in the problem, adoption was not the full answer.

Even so, almost every day we seemed to hear of another adoption agency opening its doors in Ethiopia, and the more we learned about the practice, the more we started to see that many of these agencies were in business only for the money.

American families were spending up to twenty-five thousand dollars per adoption, and much of that ended up in the pockets of executive directors and brokers who found children in remote areas and brought them to the agencies. We were grateful to be working with an agency we trusted, one we believed would do the right thing when it came to hard decisions.

"I think you're right," Jessie said after a long pause. "We need to consider how we can raise these kids in their own country. It's the only way we're going to be doing any long-term good."

We stayed up late into the night, talking in hushed voices so we wouldn't wake the kids and dreaming of new strategies. We discussed the different orphanages we'd both volunteered in around the world—some that had worked and some that had not. We agreed we'd take some time to think about our idea before talking to anyone, but overall, we both sensed a shift toward providing an in-country future for the kids.

The problem was, every direction felt wrong, and far from what we'd hoped for the children. No matter what we did, we seemed to be letting the kids down. The weight of the responsibility we'd placed on ourselves was crippling.

"It just seems we keep flip-flopping on everything," Jessie said as we continued to talk. "One day we're committed to a specific direction, and the next, we realize we were totally wrong."

"I know," I said. "But isn't that what orphan care is— learning about a child's specific needs and finding through trial and error the best way to meet those needs? Think about it: if there were a one-size-fits-all solution, there wouldn't be any more orphans. There are lots of people all over the world trying their best to provide for children, and when we talk to them, we always hear the same thing: 'Orphan care is messy business.'"

Jessie shrugged. "I know you're right. It just feels so frustrating to realize we're once again on the wrong path."

†

A shrill scream came from the small child sleeping on a foam mattress near the foot of our bed. Jessie and I shot up, and I looked around the room, confused. *Who is that?* I wondered, still in the fog of deep slumber. Slowly it came to me: Kulo was in our room. We'd arrived back in Addis late the night before to get him badly needed dental care, and Kulo had made it clear he would not go for sleeping alone.

I made my way to the foot of the bed and tried to

soothe him. Kulo had been at the orphanage only a few weeks. Although we weren't sure, we guessed he was somewhere around six or seven years old. The trauma this child had suffered created endless nightmares.

We were told Kulo had been deemed mingi because his permanent top teeth had come in before those on the bottom. He was aware that his family had intended to kill him—something that was hard for me to comprehend. The practice of mingi was something the younger children did not understand. But six- or seven-year-olds had likely seen friends, or even family members, killed. The thought of what this boy must have lived through was horrifying.

As Kulo shook violently, I held tight to his body and silently prayed for him. My heart ached as I considered the deep pain this child must be feeling. Did he know how close he had been to death? Did he understand that he'd been rescued and was now safe?

I held him tighter and talked quietly into his ear, knowing he didn't understand English, but hoping he'd feel the love. "You are safe," I said, over and over again. "You are safe."

†

It was late when my former business partner, Micah, called. Micah was easily the friend I trusted most. We'd worked well together, our skills complementing each other's in a way I'd never quite experienced before.

I walked outside and sat against the wall next to the old blue VW bug we'd recently purchased to get around town. We exchanged small talk for a few minutes, and then—for a moment—the phone went silent.

Kulo had been deemed mingi because his permanent top teeth had come in before those on the bottom. He was aware of the fact that his family intended to kill him—something that was hard for me to comprehend. Little children did not under-stand the practice of mingi. But six- or seven-year-olds had likely seen friends, or even family members, killed. The thought of what Kulo must have lived through was horrifying.

"How are you doing, man?" he asked.

I couldn't hold back the tears. "I don't know if we can go it alone anymore. We're struggling to keep our heads above water, and it feels like we're not getting anywhere," I told him, thankful for a listening ear.

"Well . . ." He hesitated. "Emily and I are thinking about coming out there with our three kids to help you guys."

I was stunned. "Are you for real?" I asked, hoping he wasn't just messing with me.

"Sort of," he said. "But there's some stuff I need to talk to you about first." His voice got quieter. "I need to talk about how you left things. I really feel like you didn't appreciate all I did to close out the business, or acknowledge what I had to do to clean things up. Levi, the truth is, I wanted to come too. I wanted to help out in Ethiopia. I believed in you, Levi. I always have. I still do. And because I believed in you, I wanted to stay behind and smooth things out so you could move forward. I just need to know that you appreciate all I did back home to make things happen for you."

I knew everything Micah said was true. After we left California, he had spent nearly six months closing out the business, dealing with angry investors and the details of leases we could not pay. Although I understood that, I had never really expressed my appreciation.

Tears rolled down my cheeks. "I'm so sorry," I said, trying to find better words to describe how I felt. The truth was, I'd always known I was a jerk for leaving him that way. And yet I'd never told him that.

"I'm sorry," I said again.

I leaned against the wall and clenched my teeth; the emotions were flowing faster than I could control. "I messed up, Micah," I told him. "I ran over here too fast and never looked back. I tried so hard to make it feel okay to neglect the details, but the reality was, even though it was too late to fix anything, I shouldn't have put you through so much by yourself."

Micah tried to speak, but his emotions got the best of him. His voice began to crack. "I understand, Levi. I just needed to hear you finally say it. That's all."

I felt horrible for not apologizing earlier. The fact was, I should have called him a long time ago. I asked his forgiveness and told him we'd love to have his family in

Ethiopia. We needed them desperately, and I was thankful he was a good and forgiving friend—a friend I didn't deserve.

✝

Without warning, the tribal winds shifted, slamming shut the fragile door between us.

One by one, calls started pouring in: "We were too late," friends close to the tribes would tell us, their voices trailing off under the gravity of the loss.

It seemed the Kara were going through a baby boom of sorts. For such a small group of people, it was incredible how many were giving birth each month—sometimes several babies a week. The problem was, the mingi children were being killed before we could get to them, and we didn't know why.

When I pressed our friends for details, they'd only whisper, "It's the elders."

Jessie and I began to dread the sound of a ringing phone: "We've lost another one," the voice on the other line would say again as we cried out to God for answers.

10

AFTER CHOWKI LEFT the orphanage, Abreham tried to adjust. He missed his mother, but at least he was still in a familiar place. He knew the other children well and was comfortable with them. Then the reality of his situation began to settle in, and Abreham decided he was not going to eat or drink. Before long, Jessie and I began getting frantic calls from the staff.

"He is getting skinny," a desperate nanny would tell us. Then a few days later another would call. "He does not have any energy left," she'd say, pleading.

Finally Jessie and I knew we had to do something. We had no idea whether we'd be able to help this desperate boy, but we had to try. We went down to Jinka to pick up little Abreham and move him in with us. We had no intention of adopting him, but we knew that something had to be done or he was going to waste away to nothing. He was only eighteen months old and had already been through far more in his short life than anyone should have to endure.

We'd asked Chowki several months earlier if Abreham could be on the list of children to be adopted, and she agreed. Consequently, Abreham was one of the kids matched with a family in America. We were pretty sure he had about three to four months to go before his new family would be allowed to pick him up.

By now, Jessie and I knew how to handle the night terrors. We allowed Abreham to sleep between us in our bed. We understood why he needed to take all the toys in the house and make them his own. We became accustomed to his screaming and inconsolable fits when something didn't go his way. We did what we needed to do: love him and be a constant in his life.

Immediately after moving into our home, it was clear that Abreham preferred me to anyone else. "That's fine," Jessie would say. "You take care of him, and I'll take care of the other kids. Besides, he's a lot more work than all four of them together," she'd add with a laugh. And she was right.

Day after day I'd strap Abreham to my back with an ERGObaby carrier and walk around the house wearing headphones in an attempt to drown out his desperate cries. For the first two weeks, he didn't seem to be making progress. Jessie and I prayed hard, hoping that soon we'd begin to see improvement.

Finally that day came.

I was reading on the couch, making sure Abreham and I were touching in some way so he wouldn't panic. Suddenly Abreham decided he wanted something across the room. He got up from the couch and walked over to get a toy. But instead of running back to me, he actually sat down and started to play. *Alone*. I focused on my book, stealing glances when he wasn't looking, amazed that we might actually be getting somewhere.

Over the next few weeks Abreham improved dramatically. He began to interact with the other kids, which allowed me more freedom. And then he started to open up to Jessie, permitting her to hold him.

We watched with joy as Abreham grew stronger each and every day.

Then the moment we'd been waiting for finally arrived: Micah, Emily, and their three children—ages two, five, and seven—joined us in Ethiopia. Our whole family was thrilled. For more than a month, we'd been counting the days until we could see our friends, and we could hardly believe they were finally here.

A few weeks before they landed, we had moved our family into a new home, one that was both cheaper and nearly double the size of our other one, although we had to give up our grassy yard in exchange for a small cement patio the size of a parking space.

It was simple, but it was home.

†

A month or so after Micah and Emily arrived, Gulo, another mother, came to live at the south orphanage. But unlike Chowki, this mother hadn't yet delivered. She was married, but because she and her husband had failed to announce their intent to conceive, their child would be deemed mingi at birth and killed.

Gulo and her husband agreed that their baby should live. They knew it was not possible for the child to stay with them in their village, so they contacted the orphanage and asked if Gulo could come there to give birth.

She had been in the orphanage only a few weeks when she asked to go to Addis to see a doctor. She was concerned that something might be wrong with her pregnancy and wanted to get an expert's opinion. We agreed that she could live with us at our home in Addis at the same time three other children in the orphanage—Musse, Gnawie, and Alma—were sick and needed to come for medical care.

Gulo brought her two-year-old daughter and another nanny. We had also hired an assistant to help out with Abreham. And so it was that our home came to house nineteen people at the same time. We were packed full!

†

Having Gulo with us was a challenge. She stared at us through cold, confused eyes. She pushed away any food we offered, shaking her head in disgust. We attempted to prepare different meals for her, but we always received the same response. When we'd gesture toward her pregnant stomach, trying to explain that she needed to eat, she'd burst out in her tribal language in fast, harsh-sounding tones.

Jessie and I wondered what to do with Gulo. Of course, we were more than happy to open our home to her; we loved the idea of a mother who was carrying a mingi child staying with us through her pregnancy. We felt her arrival was a breakthrough. Our plan was to care for this woman with the utmost patience so that she'd go back to her village and tell others that there is a better way.

But reality was setting in fast. A clash of cultures was underway inside our house, and the language barrier was only the beginning.

We discussed what we might do to help Gulo feel comfortable. "I can relate to the discomfort of pregnancy. I just want to take her for a massage or something," Emily offered with a smile.

"I wish there was something we could do to show how much we care," Jessie added.

I walked over to Gulo and asked if she was hungry, gesturing to my mouth. She shook her hand, leaned toward the wall, sucked deep in her throat, making a loud noise, like a trucker, and spewed a large green blob onto the white wall. I stepped back in shock, completely caught off guard by her behavior. Gulo looked at me and smiled. I walked into the kitchen where the others were still talking. "Oh, my gosh," I said. "You won't believe what just happened."

Over the next few weeks, we learned to communicate a little better. We discovered Gulo liked Morvite, a porridge sort of dish that was made from a powder we found at the store.

We decided it was best not to say anything about her spitting on the walls. At that point, the walls of the room she was staying in were covered with green slime. We bit our tongues and tried our best to focus on the big picture: paint was cheap. And we were saving lives. That's all that mattered.

Despite Gulo's anger, we began to notice that she liked Micah, learning to say his name and no one else's. Sometimes she'd make tea, but only for Micah.

We found a doctor with an ultrasound machine and were able to see that the baby, due in about two months, was a boy. When she heard the news, Gulo didn't smile. Clearly this birth was not going to be a joyous event. She was a mother. She had a family, a husband, and a home, but Gulo understood she couldn't care for this baby, a baby that was as much her child as her little daughter, whom she loved so dearly.

†

Emily woke up to find Gulo standing over her as she slept. "Shai," Gulo said flatly, as Emily opened her eyes.

"Huh?" Emily replied, half asleep.

"Shai," Gulo repeated before turning to walk out of the room. Emily sat up. Then it hit her: *shai* was the Amharic word for tea. *She wants to have tea with me!* Emily thought, jumping out of bed, excited that she might finally be making progress with Gulo. Emily quickly dressed and came downstairs, only to find Gulo sitting on the couch, with no tea in sight.

"Shai?" Emily asked, confused.

"Yes," Gulo said as she gestured toward the stove. Emily walked into the kitchen and, realizing the tea had not been made, put on a pot of water to heat.

After a few minutes she emerged with two steaming mugs of tea, set them on the table in front of Gulo, and reached over to grab a chair so they could share a moment together. But when Emily turned around, Gulo had taken the tea and was heading outside, where Micah was playing soccer with the kids. She watched as Gulo stood proudly in front of Micah and handed him one of the mugs.

"Thank you," Micah said innocently, as Emily giggled from a distance.

In time, Gulo felt confident that her baby was healthy and wanted to have him at a hospital in Jinka. We never really knew what was going on inside her head or why she decided to leave, but we were thankful for the opportunity to have her in our home, even if it was just for a few weeks.

†

We were plugging along when we got the call from the agency that our adoption papers were finished on the Ethiopian side and were ready for the embassy. The three American families were called and told to make travel plans. It was finally happening!

"You need to have Endale, Bale, and Goyiti brought to the transition home," Zelalem said in broken English. We really enjoyed working with Zelalem and had a great deal of respect for him.

By now, Edalawit had been living in our home for nearly a year, and we were excited to see her adoption close to finalized.

†

Two days later, we were on the road to pick up the soon-to-be-adopted children in Jinka and get them to the embassy. Micah and Emily offered to take care of our two oldest, so we only had Ruth and Edalawit in the car on the way down.

Jessie and I knew this trip would be a piece of cake. It

was the return journey we were worried about. We were picking up Endale, who was four; Bale, who was two; and Goyiti, who had just turned two. We knew from experience that Endale and Goyiti would be relatively easy—although we wished Luella could have come along. Luella had an incredibly close relationship with Goyiti and was the only person Goyiti would allow to hold her.

Bale, on the other hand, had a reputation far and wide for an "I'm the boss" attitude. We cringed at the thought of that many children in one car on such a long trip. "We can pretty much handle anything for a couple of days," Jessie kept reminding me as we drove toward Jinka.

†

We had no sooner arrived in Jinka than we were asked to sit down to discuss something important.

"The tribal people want to see the kids one more time before they leave," an interpreter told us. Seeing the concerned look on our faces, he tried to reassure us. "It's not a problem. The birth families just want to say good-bye. We need to make sure they are still okay with the adoptions."

"No problem," I said, realizing that we, too, would feel better about the adoptions if the birth families were given one more chance to see their kids before giving final approval. "Let's head out to the tribes on our way back to Addis."

We made a call to Micah and Emily and asked if they'd

be okay if we extended our trip two more days. They reassured us that our two kids were doing fine and we should do what we felt was necessary. Jessie hated the thought of leaving our children for longer than we'd planned, but we both knew this was the right thing to do.

At five the next morning we left Jinka, driving the bumpy road toward the tribes. We were thankful that for the first time since arriving in Ethiopia, we were riding in a car with air-conditioning. Imagine the hottest place on earth, and you have an idea what the summers in southern Ethiopia feel like: a furnace from morning to night.

Most of the time, the kids were relatively calm and seemed to enjoy watching the scenery. It was not until the last hour of the ride that Bale decided she wanted to climb from seat to seat. When we told her to stop, she began screaming and kicking her feet in everyone's face. Jessie and I tried our best to control her, but we quickly realized that we were going to have to let her continue to change seats or the ride was going to become unbearable. We were getting better at choosing our battles.

Finally, we arrived at a small hotel in Turmi, two hours outside of Duss—the village where Bale was born—and unloaded for the night. We planned to head out early the next morning and spend the entire day in the tribes, then sleep one more night in the hotel before making the long trek back to Addis Ababa.

✝

From the moment our car made its way between the grassy huts and into the clearing in the middle of the village, there was tension in the air. Jessie and I had asked many times if the tribe would have a problem with mingi children coming to visit, and we were told it would be okay.

But clearly, something was wrong.

One of the families immediately recognized their child. Standing back from the crowd, you could almost see a battle raging inside them. Other villagers dared to come closer, but no one touched the kids.

We were standing in the middle of a crowd that was easily a hundred strong when we noticed there was not a single man present. The women, wearing goatskin skirts and heavily adorned with colorful jewelry, were talking in loud, animated voices.

"Can you translate?" I asked the man who'd brought us.

"They say these kids are beautiful, and they cannot believe they are still alive," he replied.

"Ask them if they want to hold her," Jessie said, motioning to Edalawit, who was in her arms.

After he translated, a woman stepped forward.

"She said yes," our translator told us. "This is her aunt," he went on, as Jessie handed over little Edalawit. We stood transfixed, watching Edalawit reunite with her people, in a place she never had the chance to know before she was almost killed.

"She is even more beautiful than her mother's other children," the woman said, gesturing to Edalawit.

"Tell them to keep their next mingi child," Jessie said boldly.

He translated in a loud voice, so everyone in the crowd could hear. And immediately, there was a deafening silence.

An older woman spoke up. "I have killed many mingi children, but no more," she said.

Finally an older woman spoke up. "I have killed many mingi children, but no more," she said.

The crowd erupted in a frenzy.

I put my arm around Jessie and picked up Ruth to make sure everyone was safe. The crowd was pushing against us on all sides and making a ruckus that made me feel uneasy. *We have no idea what they're capable of*, I thought, as I tried to hold on to my family.

Just then, from the back of the crowd, Bale's parents came forward and said something that made everyone quiet down. The villagers talked back and forth for some time while we waited. This was beginning to feel like the biggest mistake we could have made. We didn't really know what they thought of us and our efforts to save their children.

Finally our translator leaned in to explain what was going on. In the distance, we saw Bale's family turn and head toward the river. "They are going to talk with the elders to see if they can take Bale home with them," he said.

Jessie and I stepped back, stunned at the news. I tried to ask what this meant, but our translator turned on his heels and walked toward Bale's family, out of sight.

The crowd continued to press hard, touching our skin and hair and asking questions that we did not understand about the kids. "Do you think they're talking about taking Bale for real?" Jessie asked, clearly as worried as I was.

"I don't know what to think," I said, scrambling for a better answer. What if Bale's mother and father came back and asked for their daughter? Could I tell them no? Could I deny them that right? And if Bale went back to her parents, would she be safe?

Then a man who spoke fairly good English appeared. "This baby would not be here if I did not save her twice," he said, stroking Edalawit's hair as Jessie held our little girl in her arms.

"Really?" Jessie said, mesmerized by his words.

"Yes," he continued. "When her mother was pregnant, the father asked me to make a mixture of roots that would put her in labor so the baby would be delivered too early to live. I said no. Later, right after the babe was born, I was walking by and saw her struggling on the ground with dirt in her mouth. I was the one who rescued this child and hid with her in a hut."

Jessie and I stood transfixed. We'd heard of this man

but had never had the chance to thank him for saving the child who was about to become our daughter.

"Thank you," I stammered, desperately wanting to say something more profound but unable to find the words.

I was overcome with a burning desire to hug this man. I reached toward him, wrapped my arms around his wiry frame, and gave him a big American bear hug—instead of the traditional Ethiopian handshake–shoulder bump. Patting Edalawit on the head, he smiled broadly.

In the distance we could see Bale's parents coming toward us once again. This time, they had a small baby with them and were heading our way in very deliberate, quick steps, approaching the crowd from the back. Immediately everyone parted, providing a direct path to us.

"The mother will spend time with Bale, but not in her own home. That is forbidden," the translator told us, motioning toward a hut that belonged to another family. "We will go there," he said.

We migrated toward the hut, and I stole a look at Jessie. She flashed me a relieved glance and whispered under her breath. "I guess we were worried for nothing," she said.

My stomach churned. We'd always wanted the kids to be reunited with their birth parents someday, and we hoped the practice of mingi would end. We discovered there was never really a discussion about taking Bale back, only talk of visiting with her for a few minutes and whether or not the elders would permit that visit in the family's own home.

Inside the hut, several women lined up along the floor. We were told the guests included Bale's mother, grandmother, and two aunts. A teenage-looking girl sat at the end of the line. When we asked if she was related, we were told she was not. However, she'd given birth a few weeks earlier, and because she was not married, the child was declared mingi. "She killed the baby," the translator said matter-of-factly. "And she is here because she is sad and wants to see another baby who was mingi but is not dead."

A teenage-looking girl sat at the end of the line. She'd given birth a few weeks earlier, and because she was not married, the child was declared mingi. "She killed the baby," the translator said matter-of-factly. "And she is here because she is sad and wants to see another baby who was mingi but is not dead."

I looked at the young girl and reached out to shake her hand. The pain was visible in her eyes as she watched Bale dance around on the mat laid out on the floor. I lost myself in thought as I tried to process the hurt she must be feeling.

Bale's mother reached toward her little girl. "Bale," she said, holding out her hand. Bale had no idea who she was. She'd been away from her mother for over a year, and if there was any memory of her, Bale did not show it.

She stopped playing for a moment, walked over to her

mother and shook her hand politely, then quickly pulled away and went back to performing somersaults on the mat. Her grandmother motioned toward Bale and said something that made all the women laugh.

Jessie ushered Bale toward her mother, assuring her it was okay. Bale shook her hand once more, then patted the head of the small baby her mother was nursing. "That's your brother," Jessie said, motioning to the tiny infant. Bale leaned down and kissed him on the forehead.

Tears formed in her mother's eyes as she stroked her daughter's cheek. "Bale," she said soothingly. "Bale."

11

THE ONLY THING BIGGER than Gnawie's beautiful round face was her heart.

Her mother was fifteen when she gave birth, and because she was not married, Gnawie had been deemed mingi. After a brutal argument that lasted for almost a year, the tribe won out. Gnawie was taken from her mother and placed in our orphanage, where her sweet demeanor quickly caught the eye of an orphanage worker's wife.

"My husband and I want to adopt her," she said one afternoon as we sat on the floor sipping coffee. Jessie and I could hardly believe our ears. We'd prayed that someone from the local community would step up and set an example for others, and now it appeared this little girl would be placed with an Ethiopian family.

But our hopes were soon dashed. Gnawie came down

with such a severe case of diarrhea that she had to spend a few days in the hospital, where her symptoms baffled the doctors and nurses. She had blood in her stools, cried uncontrollably, and ate more than any child her size should be able to put away. But despite all the medical interventions, nothing the doctors came up with seemed to work.

Finally a senior physician ordered an HIV test, knowing the basic test they had in the hospital wasn't going to be accurate for a child Gnawie's age.

Gnawie tested positive—three times in a row.

Simi called me, his voice low and sad. "Something is wrong, Levi," he said. "It's Gnawie. The doctors are sure it's HIV."

Trying to believe it was a mistake, I asked Simi to bring Gnawie to Addis for more tests. In the meantime, Jessie and I researched everything we could, calling doctors in the States, looking up infant HIV cases online, and praying something would change.

Unfortunately, additional tests revealed the same results. Gnawie was infected with HIV.

Good medical care for people with HIV was available only in Addis Ababa, and Gnawie's prospective adoptive family couldn't live there and keep their jobs at the orphanage in the south.

And that is how another orphan came to live in our home in Addis Ababa. Our house was packed, and our hearts were stretched.

We loved Gnawie and welcomed her with open arms.

But we were also realistic. Jessie and I researched ways HIV could be transferred from one person to another, bought a box of surgical gloves, and prayed we were making the right choice.

We soon became regulars at the HIV clinic, learning to reach beyond our comfort zone. Over time, we discovered that many of the fears related to HIV were unfounded. In reality, having an HIV-positive child in our home was safe, as long as we took proper precautions. We also found that living with Gnawie helped our children understand that people shouldn't be seen through a filter of disease but instead appreciated for who God created them to be.

On the flip side, in having another child in the home, we were asking our own four children to share our attention, and it wasn't easy. At times Jessie and I wondered if we were incapable of saying no. But how could we in good conscience deny any child the right to medical care?

And so, our family grew.

†

Without warning, the calls started coming, and none of them were good. Endale's adoption had stalled, and Rich and Melissa had been put on hold indefinitely.

Everyone wanted answers. Then the e-mail arrived:

> The embassy has decided to investigate our adoptions, and they are finding issues. You need to call quickly.

I was caught completely off guard. I'd thought that Rich and Melissa were about to receive Endale's entry visa so they could head back to America.

I punched in Rich's cell number.

"What's going on?" I asked as soon as he picked up the phone.

"We're not sure. Apparently, someone made a huge mistake and submitted the wrong information to the embassy. At this point, all we know is they are investigating Endale's history, and we need to sit tight."

I felt light headed. Everything seemed so out of control. Our organization had done everything right with the adoptions, everything we could to go above and beyond the usual process. Yet this was still happening—and Jessie and I felt helpless.

The connection dropped. I stumbled into the bathroom and brushed my hand up and down the wall, feeling for the switch. As the light flickered to life, I looked at myself in the mirror. I was a mess. I could hardly recognize the thin, pale reflection staring back at me.

†

Jessie and I sat down with Rich and Melissa to get the full story. It seemed someone along the way had submitted the wrong documents for Endale even though our organization had informed the courts he was considered mingi and his parents had abandoned him because of tribal superstition.

"It's going to be okay," Rich explained. "It's just that they must research the whole story since there was an inconsistency in the documentation. The court needs to meet the birth family to make sure everything is true. Hardly anyone knows about mingi in the north," he added.

Rich was right. Jessie and I found that few in Addis had ever heard about mingi, and if they had, they thought the practice had ended years ago.

Within a month the embassy and the court agreed the adoptions could move forward. However, in the process a new problem was unearthed. Although the families of mingi children in the tribes agreed with the premise of adoption and wanted their children placed in families, no one wanted the national government meddling in their lives. The tribes had lived in isolation for so many generations, having few reasons to interact with the government on any level. Now they were being asked to travel to Addis to appear in court—an experience that for them was akin to visiting Mars. In addition, the tribal people were being questioned by representatives from the United States embassy, and not one of them was comfortable with any of it.

Jessie and I were faced with a dilemma. If we continued with the adoptions, we'd lose our relationship with the tribes. If the tribal people pulled away from the scrutiny, more children would be murdered. And we did not want their blood on our hands.

We decided we had to stop processing all adoptions and come out with an immediate statement to the tribes, assuring them we'd no longer seek to adopt out any child that came to our orphanage. We called every tribal contact we had and made it known that we were changing gears. Our organization would no longer bring the government into their lives if they did not want it, even if it meant adoptions would cease.

If we continued with the adoptions, we'd lose our relationship with the tribes. If the tribal people pulled away from the scrutiny, more children would be murdered. And we did not want their blood on our hands.

The decision to stop the adoption process was a difficult choice. Jessie and I were firm believers that each and every orphan had a right to a family, and these children were clearly orphans in the fullest sense of the word. However, we also knew that because we were no longer focusing on adoptions, we'd be able to concentrate on making the orphanage a better place to live.

But before any of that could happen, I had another call to make.

†

I stayed up late into the evening and dialed the number, my hands shaking as I pressed each digit into the keypad on my computer. For the first time since we'd arrived, we were able to use Skype on our normally slow Internet connection. The phone rang a few times before it was answered. My voice shook as I explained the situation to the couple from the church in California, who'd been matched with little Abreham.

"We so desperately want him to be part of your family," I explained. "He, of all the children, needs a stable home. But we cannot risk having more children die just to give him the family he deserves."

My heart ached as the couple began to cry.

I tried to explain the complicated tribal issues we were dealing with, and even though the people were gracious and expressed gratitude for our hard work, I knew they didn't really understand why this little boy, whose picture was already framed on their mantel, could not come to live with them.

The truth was, Jessie and I cared for Abreham as much as they did. We'd even dreamed of adopting him ourselves. He was sweet and gentle, and we were in love with this two-year-old little boy. But we'd been forced to come to terms with a harsh reality: if we were going to be able to save other lives, Abreham could never have parents of his own.

†

Over the next week, Jessie and I dug in our heels. If we were unable to adopt kids out, we were going to stop at nothing to give the children a better life in the orphanage. We accepted the challenge, convinced that no matter what it took, we would make it happen. Micah and Emily worked tirelessly to do the same for the orphanage in the south. Through great dedication, and small construction projects, they took that stale old house and made it feel like a home.

We rented a beautiful compound with four bedrooms and a nice outdoor play area, then hired Ethiopian staff from the local church. Jessie and I moved the children who were staying at our house into the new orphanage in the north, struggling through the emotions of having to let go. Each of the kids had made enormous progress since arriving, but we knew if they were not going to be adopted into our family, it was best for them not to become any more attached to us than they already had.

And Jessie and I knew something more. Every action, no matter how well-intentioned, brings a definite reaction: it's often the transitions, the constant moving from place to place, that hurt orphans the most.

The children weren't the only ones experiencing transitions: after nine months in Ethiopia, it was time for Micah, Emily, and their three kids to head back to the States. As everyone tearfully hugged good-bye, we knew we'd miss them terribly, but we were grateful for good friends, opportune help, and treasured memories.

†

Seated safely in the back of the room, I slid around on my chair, admiring its sturdy metal construction. *Has to be made in America*, I thought, as I tried to pass the time. Artwork stretched high on the walls of the impressive new American embassy. The auditorium was designed to inspire awe, but it just made me feel out of place.

It had been nearly one and a half years since I'd been back to the States, and none of the architecture in Ethiopia even remotely resembled the expansive building the American embassy had finished constructing just a few weeks before this meeting had been called.

"Please take your seats. We are going to start in a minute," a short American man said as he leaned into the microphone. Roughly a hundred people in the room moved toward the empty chairs. "As you all know, we have an important agenda for today's meeting," the man said, pausing before continuing.

For the next twenty minutes, several authorities stood up to speak. Each began by mentioning the large construction project they'd just completed, thanking the various levels of government that had been involved in making it happen. I tapped my foot nervously, wondering when we might get past the pleasantries and on to the real reason the room was packed full of anxious American citizens.

Finally, the stage was handed over to a younger man

wearing a gray suit. He introduced himself as the American services director and dived into the topic we all wanted to hear about. "There's been a change in the Ethiopian government's interpretation of immigration law. We're not exactly sure when it happened," he explained flatly as everyone leaned in, listening for scraps of information.

For the past few weeks the buzz on the street had been escalating. We all knew something was wrong, but no one wanted to go to the government to find out because of the risk of showing up personally: several Americans were rumored to be in jail—for what, we had no idea. One of the largest humanitarian organizations working in the country had been thrown out completely, but all we had heard were muddy stories.

The fact of the matter was, no one really understood what was going on, only that we were at risk of being thrown in jail for crimes we didn't even know we might be committing. "If you're here on a business visa, no matter how long its term, you must now leave the country every ninety days or risk arrest," the speaker explained.

I quickly calculated how long it had been. More than ninety days. *Not good.*

"I suggest that if any of you are here on a business visa and you have been in the country longer than ninety days, you leave as soon as possible. We at the embassy can do only so much to protect you as American citizens, and the local government is not joking around with this new regulation."

I dreaded telling Jessie that once again our world had been turned upside down. We had nowhere near enough money to cover the trip back to America, but somehow we had to find it fast.

Even if we were able to make it happen this time, I wondered how our family could afford to leave the country every ninety days. There was no doubt: the work we'd committed to doing was becoming incredibly expensive.

I decided to seek additional advice. "How long do we have?" I asked at the counter through the thick plate-glass window.

"Would you like me to direct you to the jail where you can visit all the other Americans who asked me that question?" the man said, his tone so serious it sent shivers up my spine.

"So are you telling me we have to leave now?" I asked, already fearful of his answer.

"Yes, sir," he replied with absolute certainty. "And I suggest you have a buddy system with some local friends so they can make sure your family gets through the airport immigration line. They have been arresting people there as well."

"How long do we have?" I asked.

"Would you like me to direct you to the jail where you can visit all the other Americans who asked me that question?" the man said, his tone so serious it sent shivers up my spine.

I thanked him for the information and went home to talk with Jessie about how we were going to comply.

†

After looking at every option, we decided we'd need to get back to America soon, to officially straighten things out.

The problem was, getting back to the United States wasn't going to be cheap. The total for our round-trip flights was staggering: more than eight thousand dollars. Money we did not have.

"We are in a bind," I wrote on our blog, trying my best to convey the desperate situation we found ourselves in and, at the same time, not scare our families back in the States. "We need to raise money for tickets to get home, because we're not legally allowed to stay under the new law," I continued. "It's only temporary, though," I added, trying to make sure people understood we were not leaving Ethiopia for good.

And then a miracle happened.

Within ten days, all the designated money came in to purchase our flights. Every cent! Jessie and I were more than joyous. The overwhelming support seemed to assure us that our calling hadn't changed—that we were on the right path. People we'd never met, people we didn't realize cared about our work in Ethiopia, stepped up to send our family back to America in just the nick of time. Checks showed up. Large checks. Some for thousands of dollars.

I returned to the airline office and handed over my ATM card. We were going home!

12

IN OUR FRANTIC EXIT out of Africa, we almost overlooked a hidden blessing: our plane was scheduled to land in California on Thanksgiving Day.

After more than thirty hours of flight time and layovers, our four kids teetered between wild excitement and utter exhaustion. Even so, we were thrilled to arrive at Jessie's grandmother's home just in time for the festivities. After a tiring but joyous family reunion filled with tears and laughter, we loaded our plates with the delicious bounty: turkey, stuffing, buttery mashed potatoes with creamy gravy, and an assortment of homemade fruit pies.

As the excitement swirled around me, it began to sink in: our rapid departure from Ethiopia wasn't simply a legal inconvenience; it was also a divinely orchestrated gift. I closed my eyes and thanked God for the unforeseen blessing of sharing a holiday with family back home.

†

The culture shock our family experienced returning to America was at times more intense than when we first landed in Ethiopia. The cars on the freeway moved so fast that we gripped our seats in fear. And the excesses were staggering. In Ethiopia, we saw poverty all around us. In America, we observed gluttony and waste.

This was once your life too, I reminded myself. But on occasion I had to bite my tongue as I watched folks spending more money to put gas in their SUVs than it would cost to feed a family in Ethiopia for several months.

As the excitement swirled around me, it began to sink in: our rapid departure from Ethiopia wasn't simply a legal inconvenience; it was also a divinely orchestrated gift. I closed my eyes and thanked God for the unforeseen blessing of sharing a holiday with family back home.

At times I had the strange sensation that I'd grown irrelevant to my old life. I was no longer comfortable just hanging out with buddies and shooting the breeze. Our experiences had become too dissimilar, the chasm between us too wide.

I wasn't the only one feeling socially disconnected.

"No one gets me anymore," Jessie blurted out one evening, nearly in tears. "I don't know how to bridge the gap," she said.

Even our children struggled to fit in. Their best friends

now were back in Ethiopia. When they tried to share stories about wild monkeys who hung out in the yard, and long car rides into the mountains of Ethiopia, it served more to entertain their stateside friends than to spark real camaraderie.

Although our family was happy to be back in America, we were beginning to feel like outcasts in our own land.

†

We had crammed our family into two bedrooms and tried to provide a sense of stability for our children, who were beginning to ask questions about why we'd been uprooted again, why we had to leave Ethiopia in such a hurry. We did our best to explain, but for the younger ones, we tempered things a bit. We simply felt they were too young to understand. "Let's just enjoy our vacation with Nanna and Grandpa," we'd say, trying to focus on the positive.

Jessie's family was gracious. We knew we were a bother, but they never once hinted that was the case. The house was tight, and we seemed to fill every nook and cranny. Just getting from the kitchen to the front door required stepping through an obstacle course of children, shoes, and toys.

Jessie and I tried our best to remain positive, working each day at getting the proper paperwork in order so we could return to Ethiopia and the life that had been abruptly put on hold.

We called the orphanage staff often, asking about the kids and wishing with everything in us that we could return soon. Each conversation made us more determined to get the process completed so we could get on a plane and go back to where we belonged.

†

I checked my watch: 5:50 a.m. West Coast time.

The Ethiopian Embassy in Washington, DC, was scheduled to open in ten minutes, and I intended to be the first one to call as soon as they unlocked the doors. No matter what, I didn't want a repeat of yesterday's scenario, when I'd given up in frustration after two hours on hold.

I was desperate to reach the authorities. I'd mailed our passports three weeks earlier and was still waiting for visa approval, a process that was supposed to take only seven to ten days. I figured if I caught the staff as soon as they arrived, I might have a better chance of getting through.

Rechecking my watch, I prepared to dial. With one minute to go, I decided it couldn't hurt to get a sixty-second head start. But the moment the phone rang, I was placed on automated hold as the recorded voice said, "Your call will be answered in the order it was received . . ."

I had long ago memorized the three-minute recording and felt as if I might throw the phone through a wall if I had to listen to it one more time. To break the monotony, I set the cell on a nearby table. Browsing through my e-mail, I tried to ignore the message repeating itself through the scratchy speaker on my disposable, twelve-dollar phone.

I had spent nearly two hours on hold, but this time I was determined not to give up. "Even if it takes me all day," I'd told Jessie the night before, while setting my alarm. It was beginning to look as if my prediction might come true.

The kids got up and ate breakfast, and still there was no answer. In frustration I pointed my browser to a travel site and checked how much it would cost to fly out east and deal with the bureaucracy in person. Just before I hung up the phone to purchase tickets online, a voice broke through: "Ethiopian Embassy. Can I help you?"

I scrambled to gather my thoughts. "Hello?" I started out, still unable to believe I was speaking to a real live person. After identifying myself, I began to ramble as I tried my best to explain our predicament. "And the worst part is, we already had to change our flights. We were supposed to leave almost a week ago," I exclaimed, hoping for some level of sympathy. "We would have sent our passports sooner, but we were waiting for our son's documents to be renewed, so . . ." I trailed off, knowing I'd offered too much information and was only making things more complicated than they needed to be. "The point is, we really need to know where our passports are so we can get our visas," I finished, desperately hoping for help.

"Sir, I'm sorry to tell you this, but your passports appear to be lost," she said flatly.

"What?" I asked in near panic, unable to comprehend what I'd heard.

"Yes, that's correct," she said, beginning to sound a bit annoyed by my persistence.

"Is there any way to find them?" I pleaded.

"You can call back tomorrow and see if we've uncovered the documents," she said. "But I have no way of locating them now. Unfortunately, that's all the information I can give you today."

Dismissing any level of courtesy, I hung up without bothering to say good-bye.

Seeing my frustration, Jessie jumped in with her usual determination to get the worst-case scenario out there and face it right from the start. "What is the most horrible thing that could happen?" she quizzed. "Will we be stuck in limbo forever?"

"We'll get our visas eventually," I answered.

"But if not?" she asked, pausing for me to fill in the blanks.

"We're not giving up on those kids," I said, refocusing. "It might take a few weeks, but they'll find our passports and approve our visas, and we *will* get back to Ethiopia."

Jessie smiled, encouraging me to say more.

"Imagine all the children who wouldn't be alive today if we hadn't gone to Ethiopia in the first place," I reminded Jessie. And myself.

†

While we were doing our best to get out of limbo, everyone around us was gearing up for Christmas. Finally Jessie and I gave in to the reality that we weren't getting back to Ethiopia anytime soon, so we decided to put aside our frustration and focus on taking a holiday break. Besides, we needed it badly, and we were slowly realizing what a blessing it was to spend both Thanksgiving and Christmas with family when, just a few weeks before, we had no idea either was possible.

Jessie and I purchased a few small gifts and celebrated around a brightly lit tree. Of course, Jessie's parents went all out, buying the kids a flood of presents. "As long as we have them here, we're going to spoil them," Jessie's father said as he grinned over a large pile of wrapping paper that littered every inch of the living room floor.

I was thankful for our time together despite the knot in my stomach—the one that served as a constant reminder of the uncertainty of our situation. Nothing, it seemed, was ever definite. We couldn't just enjoy a vacation or stay in one place; there was always some drama hanging over us, some unknown that threatened to derail everything we were trying to accomplish.

Then one afternoon, while I sat chatting with Jessie on the porch, the call I'd been waiting for came. After I had spent more than six weeks working on our residency status, our passports, which, as it turned out, had made their way into a wrong file, were unearthed. And in only two days they arrived back in our hands, with the proper visas inserted.

Relieved and excited, we booked our flights and packed our bags, heading back to the Ethiopian adventure that had become our purpose.

†

Slowly our vehicles caravanned along the bumpy backstreets of Addis. Jessie and I were ecstatic to be joined by our friends Rich and Melissa, who also had recently returned to Ethiopia—this time to help with the work long term. The children were in high spirits, bouncing up and down in their seats and talking nonstop.

Nothing, it seemed, was ever definite. We couldn't just enjoy a vacation or stay in one place; there was always some drama hanging over us, some unknown that threatened to derail everything we were trying to accomplish.

Each morning on the way to school, the orphanage kids passed the Bora Amusement Park, the carousel and Ferris wheel beckoning them to come and play. To the children, the theme park represented the pinnacle of happiness.

And now we were finally making our way to this place of wonder.

"Go play?" Kero asked as she leaned forward from the backseat, pulling on my shirt with a little too much force.

"Yes, Kero," I promised. "We go play." Kero sat back in her seat, giggling contagiously, while the others broke into a chorus of Amharic children's songs.

I looked toward the backseat, and my heart melted. This was clearly the kids' element, right where they belonged—like one big happy family.

As the vehicles pulled into the parking lot, I opened the sliding door on the side of the van, releasing a blast of powerful excitement onto the rough gravel.

"Slow down!" I shouted, as a few of the kids took off, unsupervised, toward the entrance. "Line up alongside me," I called out, pulling them safely back into the fold.

"You all right, there?" Jessie teased, as she corralled her group of equally excited children.

"Yeah, we can do this," I said, feigning confidence. "We *can* do this."

Rich, Melissa, Jessie, and I gathered the children, purchased tickets, and joyfully entered the magical gates.

"Let's start with the carousel and go from there," Jessie suggested, pointing to the colorful herd of horses and imaginary animals encircling shiny lights and mirrors.

"Okay," I said, as we began to lift the children onto their brightly painted rides.

As the little ones rode round and round in a blur of happiness, I felt an overwhelming desire to freeze the moment and preserve it for eternity.

13

SOMETHING HAD CHANGED since we'd returned to Ethiopia.

Jessie and I couldn't put a finger on what it was, but now, each interaction with the staff felt different. There was an aura of secrecy that we just couldn't define.

The decision we'd made to stop future adoptions and focus on raising the kids in their own country was working. It had freed up money for things like mattresses, better cookware, and employee raises, which helped with morale on the ground. There were even funds to hire a local craftsman to build kitchen cabinets in the north orphanage, another guy in the south to build shelves for the children's clothes, and a third to paint the homes inside and out.

On one hand, we were progressing. The moment our family landed back in Ethiopia, we felt we were in our element. On the other hand, Jessie and I had growing concerns with the way the local organization was set up. Although on the US side of the organization we had control of the budget and could decide how money was spent, when it came right down to it, we were never really in charge of the entire project.

Because of local laws regarding tribal work, it was not legal for nonnationals to be directors, only funding partners. So, effectively, we had no final say over a project we'd given everything to take on.

But Jessie and I knew this was the only way we'd be allowed to rescue children of the tribes. When we stepped back to look at the big picture, it brought everything into perspective: kids were being saved. Organizational details paled in comparison.

†

"There's something we need to talk about," I said in a quiet tone, trying not to sound confrontational. My voice cracked as I attempted to explain my concerns. "To reassure supporters," I said, leaning over a small, rickety table on the dirt floor of a local café, "the American board needs to have the ability to audit finances."

"You can trust me," one man said as he stood up and walked away from the table.

"I hope I didn't offend you," I broke in, trying to defuse the tension and get the conversation back onto neutral ground.

"No. Nothing is wrong," another man replied stoically.

But I knew that wasn't true. Jessie and I had been in Ethiopia long enough to know that culturally the people were very passive and not open when it came to expressing their feelings. Nothing was ever as it seemed, and body language always spoke louder than words. From the moment I began the conversation—and watched staff rub their temples and exhale deeply between responses— it was clear I'd been unintentionally offensive, that I'd somehow crossed an invisible line.

In Ethiopia it's considered culturally insensitive to bring up money, and I had a clear sense that this conversation was not going well. But there was more: in my heart I also had a growing sense that this meeting was about to unleash something really, really bad.

†

Despite the fact that there were hurt feelings, we were desperate. So we had an attorney prepare a contract that gave us rights to audit project finances as well as oversee all activities. Jessie and I hated having to put together something so official sounding, but the relationship had broken down to the point where we needed to go as far as we could on paper.

Besides, at the end of the day, we knew if we didn't correct the situation, our word would mean nothing to all the hundreds of people back in America and around the world who were sponsoring the kids. Now that we were seeing things that caused alarm, we knew that if we were to continue, we'd need to demonstrate full accountability. And we were told this contract was the only way to make that happen.

We submitted the legal agreement to the local board, made up of eight tribe members, and to concerned government officials, and within a few days heard rumors of a hung vote.

About the same time, Jessie and I discovered that a couple of personnel had contacted overseas acquaintances, asking them to take over the orphanage and release us from the organization.

To this day I don't know how the story was spun, but I do know from messages we began to receive that despite everything Jessie and I had put into helping the kids, we were made out to be villains.

"You need to stop selling children," one potential supporter wrote us in an e-mail.

"Go do something productive with your lives, and leave the tribes alone," chimed in another.

I knew orphan care was difficult, but I was not prepared for anything like this. If someone had sat me down a couple of years earlier and told me about the difficulties we were going to endure in our efforts to rescue children, I would have never believed it. *Never.*

We felt our world unraveling. We hoped and prayed for positive change. But things only got worse. We wondered

if something could be done to rescue the failing relationships. But the truth was, we didn't fully understand what
was going on or exactly why the
local board was pulling away.

*"You need to stop
selling children," one
potential supporter
wrote us in an e-mail.*

It was clear from their actions
that they wanted us to let go of
financial accountability. Although
we loved the children very much,
and would have given our lives
for them, we could easily see that
an agreement like this would last
only a short time. No one would

*"Go do something
productive with your
lives, and leave the
tribes alone," chimed
in another.*

continue to support an organization with this sort of
structure in place. To protect our supporters, we had to
stand our ground and insist on getting the contract signed
before we would fund anything more. The decision was
an easy one: we would have integrity, no matter the cost.

†

"Do you think it's possible someone else will step up
and fund the project?" Jessie asked as we sat on the park
bench of a local hotel while our four kids played on the
swings nearby.

"I'm not sure," I said, wrestling with the possibilities. For the time being, we were still working with the
children and raising all the funds for the orphanages and
rescues. But with each passing day, we were feeling more

and more squeezed out. From the attitude we were getting from the local staff, it appeared our worst nightmare was coming true. Maybe the responses the staff were getting from other supporters gave them confidence that they no longer needed our participation.

"We both know it's not going to work," Jessie added. Her eyes were bloodshot. There was no doubt: the stress was testing our marriage at its very roots. Although we were still holding together, I was not sure how much more we could take.

While Jessie and I waited for the staff's decision, we tried to maintain a sense of normalcy. One afternoon while we sat on the floor of the orphanage, each holding a child on our laps, Jessie read *The Cat in the Hat* with dazzling intonation. The children giggled and pointed to the pictures.

"Cat," Mago said, her arm wrapped tightly around Jessie's neck, and a big smile spreading across her tiny face.

A few minutes later, Nickoli came in with a soccer ball and called for the kids to start a game. The children jumped up and quickly followed him to the courtyard.

Jessie and I looked at each other. I could see the pain in her eyes. Our hearts ached as we talked through what might become of the kids if they were removed from our lives. I made my way to Jessie, leaned over her, and kissed the top of her head.

At least we're still a family, I thought. *No matter what happens, we'll still have that.*

†

"Our relationship is cut off."

The words in the short e-mail sliced through my heart as I read them again and again, searching for some hidden meaning.

The message continued, explaining that the locals had voted to work with new funding partners. Then it dived into the part that hurt the most: we were no longer allowed to visit the children.

I felt as if I'd been clubbed over the head.

I closed my laptop and walked into the kitchen, where Jessie was stirring a pot of spaghetti. "It's over," I whispered, as the spoon slipped from her fingers into the vessel of boiling water.

†

"Can we go see our friends?" our three-year-old daughter, Ruth, asked for the fifth time that day. Jessie and I tried our best to explain that we could no longer visit the children at the orphanage—children who were her friends. Children who lived just a short walk from our home.

Although as our oldest, Nickoli understood the most, he was still confused. Jessie and I tried to explain that sometimes people make choices we wish they hadn't.

"The children are safe," we reassured him after talking with some of the staff and hearing that although the separation had been difficult for the kids emotionally, they were being well cared for.

†

"Your mistakes were made in the first few weeks of your arrival," an American man with decades of Ethiopian experience explained to us over coffee. "When you failed to put a contract in place before the first support came through, the problems were set in motion."

Struggling to accept the fact that we might be responsible for this mess, I gave him a perplexed look.

The words in the short e-mail sliced through my heart as I read them again and again, searching for some hidden meaning. The message explained that the locals had voted to work with new funding partners. Then it dived into the part that hurt the most: we were no longer allowed to visit the children.

"I'm not saying it's your fault," he said, trying to console us. "I'm just saying you really had no way of knowing, and by the time you figured it out, it was too late. The real question is," he continued, "what are you going to do now that you know this? Are you going to go back to America, where everything you've learned here is irrelevant, or are you going to take your new understanding and put it to good use?"

Jessie and I exchanged glances. We knew he was right, but deep down we were still heartbroken, still too wounded to move forward.

†

While my family adjusted, I struggled with a loss of identity. Over the last couple of years, my existence had become wrapped up in the rescue of mingi children. The tribal work had evolved into more than a calling. It had come to define who I was as a person.

Not wanting to leave a single stone unturned, Jessie and I made a trip back to Jinka to talk with government officials and tribal leaders and to see if there was any way we could help.

That trip was eye opening. We met an Ethiopian family who'd been taking in mingi children for the past fifteen years. We also learned that the rumors we'd heard were true: since we arrived two years earlier and began rescuing kids and raising awareness, the government had become alerted to the mingi practice and had stepped up to stop the killings. Although the horrible tradition had not ended, the officials were now taking a social-services role in the region. All rescues were now happening through the government, and within the month, a new law would take effect that prohibited rescues by private organizations.

Despite wanting more than anything to continue our

work with the tribes, we had to face the hard fact that there was no longer a need for a foreign-run organization in the area to rescue mingi children. Jessie and I prayed long and hard about the situation, and even though every fiber of our being stood up in protest, we came to the difficult realization that our mission had changed direction.

We *had* made a difference, but now the work was in the hands of the government, and mingi children would be placed in several orphanages in the area. Even though we still wanted to help, there was no way we could. Jessie and I simply brought more drama and complications than value to the work. It was as if our family itself had now been labeled mingi. So, for the good of the children in the orphanage, we made the painful decision to step aside.

And it broke our hearts.

14

I STARED AT THE PLATE of lumpy eggs. I hadn't eaten in days.

"Can we go see the kids today?" Luella asked.

"No, honey," Jessie told her, her blue eyes reflecting sorrow. "We can't see them anymore."

"Why not?" Luella almost begged. She slid a small helping of the whitish Ethiopian eggs onto her dish.

"It's hard to explain," Jessie whispered, trying her best to offer comfort.

I sat motionless, wondering if I should jump in, but I couldn't come up with a single positive word to contribute. How could I possibly explain to Luella, or to myself for that matter, the deep sorrow Jessie and I were experiencing?

As much as possible, we attempted to maintain a certain level of normalcy. Each morning Jessie helped the kids with their schoolwork. Math, English, and science lessons helped to keep our children relatively distracted. But although Jessie and I tried to remain upbeat, we were clearly losing that battle.

The reality was that things were bad. Jessie and I had not only lost the children at the orphanage; we were also wrestling with the problem of what to do next. Should we stay in Ethiopia, travel to another country, or head back to America to start a new business? We were at a loss for direction.

†

I spent the next several days researching what was happening in the tribes. The news confirmed what we'd been told on our last trip to Jinka: the government was now taking an active role in the rescues. Police were patrolling the tribal areas, and the laws were clearer: anyone who killed a child would be thrown in jail.

Belief in mingi had not changed, and the tribes were still afraid to keep children they believed were cursed, but they were now encouraged to relinquish the children, unharmed, to government officials. Once the children had been safely surrendered, the government placed them in orphanages that had sprung up in the surrounding villages.

Although we'd once been one of only a few organizations that existed to help mingi children, there were now several, some even receiving funds from government and other local sources. There were good, honest people stepping in to help the kids, and in many cases, they were backed by a large network of churches—some that had been in existence before we came but now, with the backing of new laws, were empowered to make a real difference.

I'll never know all the details of our impact, but I know one thing for sure: we had helped to save children who would otherwise be dead, and the future was looking brighter for the people of the tribes in southern Ethiopia. For that, I am grateful.

The initial need that had caused our family to move to Ethiopia was real, but the season in which we could be productive in assisting with rescuing mingi children had come to a close. Although Jessie and I loved the tribes, our relationships with key leaders had broken down. It was time to let go.

Jessie and I talked over everything, discussing in detail what we could do if we were to continue to work in the south, and in what areas we might offer help. Yes, there were some things we could do, but it was clear that we could be more effective elsewhere.

> *I'll never know all the details of our impact, but I know one thing for sure: we had helped to save children who would otherwise be dead, and the future was looking brighter for the people of the tribes in southern Ethiopia. For that, I am grateful.*

In fact, we were pretty sure where we could offer the most help. Another kind of project was coming together in our minds, one we felt would be a revolution in the way developing countries provided care for orphans.

†

I sat on the edge of the bed, nervously waiting for the phone to ring. It was only two minutes past eight in the evening, but I was already wondering if I had the wrong time or if the network was down. Jessie and I had spent the last few days gathering our thoughts on the closure of the US nonprofit organization that had been established to support the mingi orphanage. We'd sent e-mails to the stateside board members, trying our best to explain why we believed our role with mingi children had changed.

I tapped my bare foot on the floor impatiently. Even though I had a feeling the board would agree with our decision, the conference call that was coming made it all seem so final. The closing of a chapter. The death of a ministry.

I grabbed the phone on the first ring. It was Steve Gregor—the man who'd made the fateful call nearly two years earlier, asking me to make a brief trip to Ethiopia. "Hey, Steve," I said, glad to hear his voice on the other end of the line.

"How are things going, Levi?" he asked calmly. Steve was more than just a board member for the stateside organization; he had been a source of strength for Jessie and me during our time in Ethiopia. Over the last several months, he'd spent countless hours on the phone, helping us process the ups and downs.

"We're okay," I said, truly meaning those words for the first time in nearly a month.

"I'm glad to hear that," he said joyfully. We exchanged pleasantries for a moment, and then Steve broke in. "We should add the other board members on the call now." He clicked on his Skype connection, and within a few moments, all the other board members were on the line as well.

"Thank you for taking time to talk," I said, diving in nervously. "I know this is tough for everyone because we've all given so much to the mingi children. This is an important call, and I'm glad you're all here."

First up was Rich, who made it clear that he and Melissa wanted to stay in the south. They'd made connections with leaders from the local church and with directors from one of the existing orphanages, and felt doors had opened for them to serve alongside them and help advance the gospel among the tribal people.

I, on the other hand, had different news: Jessie and I planned to leave the south, but we were determined to continue working with orphans in Addis Ababa. I described our hopes for the future; then we moved on to why the call had been made: we needed to decide what to do about the organization that we had built, the one we all wanted to continue but knew had to end. It was agreed that we would shut everything down.

After thanking everyone for their understanding and saying good-bye, I walked downstairs to where Jessie was sitting on our flowered couch. "It's over," I told her solemnly. She stood up and wrapped her arms around me in a strong embrace.

†

In room after room, babies—each of them a person, a little soul—lay in rows of cribs. But in this government-run orphanage, they were held and handled only long enough to change their diapers. I stood by a crib with bent, rusty legs that caused the mattress to slope awkwardly, and reached out to touch the little girl's hand. She looked as if she might be a year old, yet she hardly moved. The back of her head was flat from resting on the mattress for so long. Slowly she extended her hand and wrapped her tiny fingers around one of mine. A smile made its way across her face.

I tried to keep it together, but I knew that if I was going to maintain any level of composure, I was going to have to get out of there fast. I disengaged my finger and moved through the room, fighting off a growing desire to take each child home.

I talked with the staff about the need for more sustainable orphan care. Just as I was learning about the scarcity of beds and funding, a woman from the police department walked through the front door holding a baby who looked no more than a few hours old.

"He was left at the hospital," she said, handing the infant to one of the staff members. Abruptly she headed out again to answer a call about another abandoned baby.

From the orphanage I drove across town to our friends Jerry and Christy's day-care project. I arrived just in time to see mothers returning from a hard day's work, where they often earned less than a dollar, to pick up their children—kids who, in many cases, would be taken back to the streets that were their home.

I watched one mother with her son. He looked about five, had cerebral palsy, and couldn't walk. She wrapped his long body in a blanket and lifted him onto her back, where he would spend the rest of the day. Off to the side, her three-year-old daughter waited patiently. It was clearly a drill they knew well.

A few hours later I went home to spend time with my family. But I couldn't stop thinking of those little children, many the ages of my own kids. I walked into the bathroom, splashed cold water on my face, and tried to forget what I had seen.

†

It was ten o'clock. I placed a few bills and my ID under my sock and reached for the ringing phone. I heard Yabi's voice. "Are you ready?"

"Yes. I'll meet you in a minute," I promised, kissing Jessie good-bye and heading out the door.

Yabi had parked the car a few minutes up the road. Along the outside wall of a big Orthodox church were teenagers and young children. Some were covered with sheets and blankets, others had only newspapers. A few dogs came alert as we walked past.

One boy, who looked eleven or twelve, sat up and smiled. "Salam no," I greeted in Amharic as I shook his hand. Yabi stepped in to translate, asking the boy about his life. My Amharic had been improving from the classes I was taking, but not enough to carry on conversations of any depth.

The boy told us he was born in a town just outside Addis. His entire family had died from illness and lack of food. After they passed away, he came to Addis to find work. But since arriving, he had been reduced to begging for money, and now lived by the church with hundreds of other boys with similar stories.

"It is hard," he told us.

Another boy stood to greet us. He was smaller and couldn't have been more than nine. He smiled a toothy grin, then laid down again on the concrete. At first I thought he was just tired, but as I watched him grip his chest and labor to suck in every breath, I realized he was sick.

A crowd began to gather, and Yabi made the call that it was time to leave. "It's not safe anymore," he said quickly, turning toward the car. "We need to go now."

I stepped away and followed Yabi, leaving much

sooner than I wanted and unable to get my mind off the dark existence the boys were forced to endure.

"Where are all the girls?" I asked as we drove away.

"Many are sold," Yabi said, his voice beginning to shake.

"*Sold?*" I asked.

"I have heard girls are being trafficked out of the country," he almost whispered. "Nobody seems to know what happens to them once they are gone."

†

Everywhere I turned, the evidence was overwhelming. The need for orphan care in Ethiopia is staggering. International adoptions are great when they're done right, but only a small percentage of orphans are ever adopted out of country. Local adoptions are a good option, but because of cultural and financial restraints, few children are taken in by Ethiopian families.

Over the last twenty years many orphanages have sprung up in Ethiopia. Several do an excellent job of preparing children to successfully enter adulthood. The problem is, all those orphanages are overwhelmed by the sheer demand for their services. Because of the lack of available space, small children have no place to go and are often left to roam the streets.

Fortunately, Jessie and I feel most at home in a mud house with kids running around our feet. We like digging in and getting our hands dirty. Because officials were

The need for orphan care in Ethiopia is staggering. International adoptions are great when they're done right, but only a small percentage of orphans are ever adopted out of country. Local adoptions are a good option, but because of cultural and financial restraints, few children are taken in by Ethiopian families.

aware of our work in Ethiopia, they began encouraging us to open a large orphanage in Addis Ababa.

Chomping at the bit to get things rolling, we spent endless hours researching the best care-home models we could find. Some were shining examples of how things should be done, and others—many others—were horrible failures that served as gateways through which children ended up back on the streets once they became teenagers. From what we had observed, orphanages broken up into small, foster-care-style units seemed to work best.

After coming up with the name *Bring Love In*, Jessie and I jotted down a vision plan:

- Bring Love In would be made up of multiple small homes, each led by a widow foster mother.
- Bring Love In would do more than give homes to children; it would also provide jobs and homes to women who were widows or whose husbands had abandoned them.
- Bring Love In would work with social workers

and a network of staff to ensure that each and every child received the best possible care and nutrition.

- Bring Love In would give the children a solid spiritual and social foundation so they would be prepared to become future leaders in their homeland.
- Bring Love In would place each child in a good school and an after-school program, where their academic and personal development would be monitored on a daily basis.
- Over time, Bring Love In would raise children across Ethiopia in a loving environment and give them the opportunity to become productive citizens.

With our vision plan set, Jessie and I geared up for the long haul of licensing, completing paperwork, and applying for funding. I knew from experience that the process would be difficult, but I also knew that if the orphanage was to be successful, we'd need more than a vision plan. I'd need to regain my sense of joy.

That evening while my family was sleeping, I stepped outside, gazed into the darkness, and asked God for a blessing: before I could move forward with Bring Love In and our plan for offering orphans hope for their future, I'd need to find hope for mine.

†

I picked up my phone and punched in the number for my friend Jerry. "Do you have time to hang out for a while, grab a bite to eat, and talk?" I asked the minute he answered.

Jerry, his wife, Christy, and their four kids had moved to Ethiopia a few years earlier and had been through their own whirlwind of struggles. I figured if anyone could understand, it would be Jerry.

"Sure," he said. "Let's do it tonight."

After we had decided on a small café, I hung up the phone and told Jessie the news. "He's going to meet me this evening," I said, with the first sign of hope I'd expressed in days.

"Be sure to tell him everything." Jessie looked deep into my eyes, as if searching for an honest reply.

"I will," I promised. Jessie was right. If I didn't open up to somebody soon, I was going to burst.

†

I boarded a taxi filled with residents of Addis Ababa making their way home from work. The van, designed for twelve people, was easily carrying twenty. Wedged tightly in the backseat, I was overwhelmed by the smell of sweaty bodies.

When I arrived at the restaurant, I found Jerry already

seated. I pulled up a chair, and we spent the next few minutes exchanging niceties: the taxi ride, new items on the menu, the approaching rainy season.

Then my words came tumbling out. "I have no idea why my family is still in Ethiopia. Now that we're not working with mingi kids, I'm not even sure who I am anymore."

Jerry nodded, smiling slightly. "Have you shared your feelings with God?" he asked.

"Well, . . . yes . . . ," I said, knowing in my heart that wasn't exactly true. "I've spent some time praying," I told him, with just a hint of defensiveness.

"Do you believe God let you down?" Jerry persisted, gently steering me toward an honest response. A tear formed at the edge of my eye, and I leaned back in my chair, trying to hold on.

But Jerry had hit the nail on the head. Although I didn't want to admit it, I *did* feel that God had let us down. Worse yet, I felt He had let the kids at the orphanage down.

For weeks I'd been trying to keep it all together emotionally. But the reality was, I didn't want to keep it together any longer. I wanted to scream and yell and throw furniture!

"You need to be completely honest, Levi. God already knows what you're thinking," Jerry said, half chuckling. "When we came to Africa, I had it all figured out," he went on. "I was going to fulfill my burning desire to change the world. After a few months in Ethiopia and some serious disappointments, it was obvious things weren't going to happen my way. God had other plans for my family, and I have to admit, I hated that."

I was grateful that Jerry really understood.

"Honestly, those were some of the darkest days of my life," he went on. "But do you know what? It wasn't until I rented a small hotel room where I could be alone for two days that I was able to really sort it out. I brought a notepad and used it to journal."

Although I didn't want to admit it, I did feel that God had let us down. Worse yet, I felt He had let the kids at the orphanage down. For weeks I'd been trying to keep it all together emotionally. But the reality was, I didn't want to keep it together any longer. I wanted to scream and yell and throw furniture!

Jerry paused when our food arrived, and then continued. "I have to tell you, Levi, I hope no one else ever finds that journal, because I put some of my deepest, most painful thoughts on paper. I laid it all on the line in that dingy hotel. I even screamed at God for what I felt was His failure. I had given up everything to help others. And it wasn't just me: my wife and four kids now lived in Ethiopia of all places, and we didn't even own a couch back in America anymore.

"I thought God screwed up big time, Levi," Jerry told me, "and I was furious. But after I told Him everything, after I shared my innermost feelings, God showed me He'd always been in control and He still had a plan."

I exhaled. Deep inside I knew Jerry was right. Yes,

I had prayed. But I hadn't been totally honest with myself. Or with God. I wasn't trusting that He knew the outcome from the beginning and He loved the mingi kids more than I ever could.

†

Jessie and I sat with our backs against the bamboo head-board. If we were going to move forward, we'd have to be real.

I looked at my wife. She was strong, but she'd been weakened by this "war." I could see our struggle reflected in her eyes. More than anything else, we both needed to release everything. We clasped hands and began to pray—slowly at first, but within moments, it poured out like a flood.

We told God the truth: we were defeated and didn't know how to get up off the floor. We were angry and con-fused; we felt cheated and trapped in a dead-end situation.

And then, after praying for the orphans by name and asking God for the future we knew they deserved, Jessie and I fell asleep in a puddle of tears.

†

The sun peeked through the thin curtains. I looked at my wife sleeping next to me and smiled. We'd done it. Together we'd braved the storm. We had been driven into the deepest, scariest places of our hearts and had come out on the other side, not only alive but changed for the better.

This was a new day, the chance to start fresh.

I began to think back to who we were when we first came to Ethiopia. Everything that had cluttered our vision and held back our faith was gone. Where we were once motivated by the drive to succeed, we were now filled with passion to help others. Selfishness had been replaced by genuine, open hearts and the near painful realization that it was never our efforts that God needed. We were broken now, and that was just how He wanted us.

I thought of the more than thirty mingi children who had been rescued. I reflected on the beautiful times we'd shared, and released them. "They are yours," I said under my breath, placing their futures in God's hands.

I was beginning to grasp just how much all of us need mercy, something we were never able to truly comprehend from the comfortable leather couch in our color-coordinated living room in California. Jessie and I were changing. Our very cores had been taken apart, piece by piece, and then gently stitched back together into something new. Something better. Something worthy of service.

I rose to my feet and slowly moved the curtain aside. As light filled the room, so did clarity: God had been there from the beginning—from that very first phone call asking me to take a leap of faith and help a tribe in Africa. Without the heartache and painful lessons of the past two years, we would never have grown; and what we'd once perceived as a series of detours was actually the road we were intended to travel all along.

I crossed the room and gently kissed my sleeping wife on the forehead. Then, careful not to wake anyone, I threw on some clothes and slipped out the door for my morning walk.

I was moving briskly down the sidewalk—the scorching sun already beating on my head—when we crossed paths. His pants were ripped and stained, and his shirt was torn and grubby, as if he hadn't taken them off in years.

Waving a crooked stick back and forth in front of him, he felt his way across the rocky earth.

His eyes were gone. Not closed. Not covered. Gone.

And then I heard his voice: he was singing. Not just any sort of song—it was beautiful, like an angelic lullaby.

I was beginning to grasp just how much all of us need mercy, something we were never able to truly comprehend from the comfortable leather couch in our color-coordinated living room in California. Jessie and I were changing. Our very cores had been taken apart, piece by piece, and then gently stitched back together into something new. Something better. Something worthy of service.

Captivated, I slowed my pace to match his and walked side by side with him. For the first time in weeks I was experiencing the absolute splendor of the world around me: the vivid African sky, the brilliant sunlight nurturing the bright green rows of maize as they stretched upward toward the heavens.

My spirit leaped. I wanted to thank this man for sharing such an amazing gift, for revealing what I hadn't been able to grasp on my own: he didn't need physical eyes to see beauty, to find direction or purpose. Nor did he need a flawless life to attain bliss.

As we came to a cross street, the man rounded the corner. For a moment I considered following him. Instead, with renewed hope in my heart, I picked up my pace and headed for home. Singing.

Epilogue

IT'S ETHIOPIAN NEW YEAR'S EVE. I'm sitting on my bed here in Addis Ababa, struggling to find the words to explain the transformation God has brought to our family. I already know that I'm bound to fail. No words, no sentence I'll ever write, will come close to painting a true picture of this journey, its struggles, its joys. Far beyond what I can capture in writing is a God who's bigger than this world, and His plan, one that's beyond our understanding. Yet I'm compelled to try—because this story is His, a story of redemption and love, one only He could write.

My hope is that as you read these words, you'll feel the true thankfulness I have for His love and direction. God could have left me where I was. He should have, but He didn't.

On the bed next to me, Jessie is asleep—exhausted from a long day's work and the effects of a sickness that's been passed from person to person in our family for the past two weeks.

The power is out again—a phenomenon that's become normal around our home at night. For now, our room is illuminated only by the soft glow of my computer screen, accompanied by the quiet sounds of a lone generator from the one house on our block where the owner can afford such luxury.

In the distance I hear excited shouts and the occasional blast of fireworks. On what would normally be a quiet Sunday evening, outside our home there's a bustling celebration. Everyone, it seems, has come to prepare for the countdown that will take place in a few hours: the entire country getting ready to ring in a new beginning with great anticipation.

As I rise from the bed to gaze out the window, I see neighbors who've gathered in song around tall bonfires, the resulting smoke accumulating in plumes and hanging low over the tin roofs and power lines. I watch as a group of children pass by our house, singing a song I cannot understand. In the neighbor's yard, I see a freshly killed sheep hanging from a tree branch and a man carving pieces of meat from its bones.

I stand at the edge of the balcony and watch as the scenes pass by, mesmerized by the curious images that surround my life. Ethiopia is a place that is home—and yet, not home at all.

This is where we live, where we serve, where we raise our kids. Except, it's not where we came from, nor does it look anything like the life we planned.

I am thankful to be here, but I'm still aware of the epic irony that's become our existence, and of the bigness that is our God. If you had asked me five years ago where I'd be today, I would never have imagined the scene displayed before me tonight.

We were the senders—the ones who stayed behind and supported others so they could go, so they could serve. We were not the ones who moved to faraway lands. That was for other people. People who were more capable. People with more faith.

Our role was to remain in America and make money so we could supply the needs of those working in the trenches. Besides, business was good. We were comfortable. How could we go?

But as I stand here at this window, listening to the sounds from the street, sounds that would have once been so foreign, so uncomfortable, I realize God has changed me, transformed me entirely, from deep inside.

In this moment of epiphany, as I contemplate the things He's done in my heart, the changes He planned and orchestrated, I realize something powerful:

I asked for this.

Before all this happened, before I turned into the guy who was willing to sell everything and move his family to Ethiopia, back when I was someone else, I asked God for this transformation.

"Change me!" I had cried out, as deep, searing pain enveloped my life.

My brother had just committed suicide. The pain of his lifestyle overcame him on a particularly dark night, taking him from this world. Forever.

My best friend had died. His liver failed, a rare disease stealing him from his wife and daughters.

My business had imploded; the success and recognition I had once enjoyed were gone.

And in the middle of that pain, in the darkness of that season, I cried out to God. Right there in the center of my failure and disappointment, I gave them over to Him like a wounded child, pleading for help.

"Change me! Do what you must, but do not stop working on me until I am wholly and completely yours."

God never forgot that prayer.

This world fails. But God persists. He calls from the gate at the start of the narrow road, beckoning us to follow.

From this strange and foreign land, I continue to travel that road—the one I asked for but did not understand. I am thankful that God answered my prayer and is continually changing me from the inside, enabling me to finally say,

I am a rescued man.
A thankful man.
A forgiven man.
A changed man.
A sold-out-for-Him man.
And He is good.

A Note to Readers

WE ARE MADE FOR MORE. Every single one of us.

Together we make up God's plan to change the world.

But what do we do with this knowledge? Made for more, yes. The answer for each of us is different.

For our family, it's orphan care. We were meant to give our lives providing orphans with hope and a future.

At Bring Love In, we're crafting a structure that will offer love, good homes, and an education to orphans while also providing jobs, homes, and economic stability for widows.

Bring Love In is a community—not just a program or an organization—a community that spans the oceans, stretches across borders, and builds bonds between people from all walks of life.

It's a community that gives more than it takes.

A community of widows who will lovingly raise children not their own.

A community of people rising up to meet the needs of orphans crying out to be loved.

Think for a moment what you'll gain from a fiery passion burning in your heart, a passion to stand up and believe, *I was made for more!*

Will you take a leap of faith and be part of this community? You are wanted here.

Follow our progress at www.BringLove.in.

About the Authors

LEVI BENKERT cares for orphans in Addis Ababa with his wife, Jessie, and their four children: Nickoli, Luella, Ruth, and Edalawit (Everly). *No Greater Love* is Levi's first book. You can reach him at Levi@bringlove.in.

CANDY CHAND is a writer living in Rancho Murieta, California. *No Greater Love* is her seventh book.